POWERSHELL AND GET-WMIOBJECT

Just when you think it couldn't get crazier than it already is!

Richard Thomas Edwards

CONTENTS

Proof is in the output
Bye, bye Get-WMIObject

*When someone changes course, they better have a
good reason for it.
--Richard T. Edwards*

HARBOR THE BELIEF THAT WHEN SOMETHING WORKS, IT DOESN'T NEED A COMPLETE REPLACEMENT. So, when GWMI aka Get-WMIObject was being superseded - starting in Windows PowerShell 3.0 - by Get-CimInstance. I started pulling out the party favors!

Didn't see that one coming, did you?

So, why am I so ready for Get-WMIObject to be retired?

Because when I write:

$objs = GWMI –namespace root\cimv2 –class Win32_Process

I get a collection of objects. But when I writer:

$objs = GWMI –namespace root\cimv2 –class Win32_BIOS

I get a collection of Properties. Why is that a problem?

Because, unless I'm trapping for the $objs count, I don't know ahead of time whether the return object is a collection or not and then, I must deal with two branches of code logic to get the job done. Not one. Below, is an example of what I mean:

```
$objs = GWMI -namespace root\cimv2 -class Win32_Process
if(! $objs.Count)
{
   Write-host "Properties"
   $obj = $objs
   foreach($prop in $obj.Properties)
   {

   }
}
else
{
   Write-host "Objects"
   foreach($obj in $objs)
   {
      foreach($prop in $obj.Properties)
      {

      }
   }
}
```

It Returned Objects

```
$objs = GWMI -namespace root\cimv2 -class Win32_BIOS
if(! $objs.Count)
{
    Write-host "Properties"
    $obj = $objs
    foreach($prop in $obj.Properties)
    {

    }
}
else
{
   Write-host "Objects"
   foreach($obj in $objs)
   {
```

```
    foreach($prop in $obj.Properties)
      {
      }
    }
}
```

It Returned Properties

So, from this, you can see what I and everyone else wanting to write code logic for this one head to deal with. The most reasonable solution to work the information was to put the data into two arrays so that a single array for names and a single array for values could be used to work the reports.

Which is exactly what we are about to do. But first, let's cover what Get-WMIObject can accept.

Some of the command line variables you can add

Not all are needed or necessary

When you run get-help get-WMIObject, a lot of crazy looking information fills the screen. Some of those command line variables you will never use. Some, you will want to use. So, let's look at the ones I find- I'm hoping you will too – worthwhile using. These are:

    -ComputerName
    -Namespace
    -Class
    -Authentication
        Default
        None
        Connect
        Call
        Packet
        PacketIntegrity
        PacketPrivacy
        Unchanged
    -Impersonation
        Default
        Anonymous
        Identify
        Impersonate

Delegate
-Locale
-EnableAllPrivileges

If you are running this call locally, you don't have to specify a computer name.

Except for -class and -namspace (if you are going to something other than the default which is root\cimv2) everything else is optional. Furthermore, there 237 locales – see Appendix B for the entire list – that you can use.

Unlike the COM version of this call, you can only set the -EnableAllPrivileges to $true or $false.

So, when I'm just testing code, my call, looks like this:

```
$objs = get-WMIObject -class Win32_BIOS
```

When the boss is looking over my shoulder:

```
$objs = get-WMIObject -ComputerName "." -Authentication PacketPrivacy -Impersonation Impersonate -Locale MS-0409 -class Win32_BIOS
foreach($prop in $objs.Properties)
{
write-host $prop.Name
}
```

And PowerShell spits out:

```
BiosCharacteristics
BIOSVersion
BuildNumber
Caption
CodeSet
CurrentLanguage
Description
IdentificationCode
InstallableLanguages
InstallDate
LanguageEdition
ListOfLanguages
Manufacturer
```

Name
OtherTargetOS
PrimaryBIOS
ReleaseDate
SerialNumber
SMBIOSBIOSVersion
SMBIOSMajorVersion
SMBIOSMinorVersion
SMBIOSPresent
SoftwareElementID
SoftwareElementState
Status
TargetOperatingSystem
Version

I'm happy with the results but to finish the job, I also need values. So, I wrote this:

```
function GetValue
{
  param
  (
  [string]$Name,
  [object]$obj
  )
  [string]$PName = "`t" + $Name + " = "
  [string]$tempstr = $obj.GetText(0)
  $pos = $tempstr.IndexOf($PName)
  if ($pos -gt 0)
  {
   $pos = $pos + $PName.Length
   $tempstr = $tempstr.SubString($pos, ($tempstr.Length - $pos))
   $pos = $tempstr.IndexOf(";")
   $tempstr = $tempstr.SubString(0, $pos)
   $tempstr = $tempstr.Replace('"', "")
   $tempstr = $tempstr.Replace("}", "")
   $tempstr = $tempstr.Replace("{", "")
   $tempstr = $tempstr.Trim()
   if($tempstr.Length -gt 14)
   {
```

```
        if($obj.Properties.Item($Name).Type -eq 101)
        {
         [System.String]$tstr = $tempstr.SubString(4, 2)
         $tstr = $tstr + "/"
         $tstr = $tstr + $tempstr.SubString(6, 2)
         $tstr = $tstr + "/"
         $tstr = $tstr + $tempstr.SubString(0, 4)
         $tstr = $tstr + " "
         $tstr = $tstr + $tempstr.SubString(8, 2)
         $tstr = $tstr + ":"
         $tstr = $tstr + $tempstr.SubString(10, 2)
         $tstr = $tstr + ":"
         $tstr = $tstr + $tempstr.SubString(12, 2)
         $tempstr = $tstr
       }
      }
      for($x=0;$x -lt $tempstr.Length; $x++)
      {
         if($tempstr[$x] -gt [char]120)
         {
            $tempstr[$x] -eq [char]32
         }
      }
      return $tempstr
     }
     else
     {
      return ""
     }
   }


    $objs = get-WMIObject -ComputerName "." -Authentication PacketPrivacy -
Impersonation Impersonate -Locale MS-0409 -class Win32_BIOS
    foreach($prop in $objs.Properties)
    {
      $value = GetValue $Prop.Name $objs
      $tstr = $prop.Name + ": " + $value
      write-host $tstr
    }
```

And what I get back is this:

```
BiosCharacteristics    : 7, 11, 12, 15, 16, 17, 19, 23, 24, 25, 26, 27, 28, 29, 32, 33,
40, 42, 43, 50, 57, 58, 64, 65, 66, 67, 68, 69, 70, 71, 72, 73, 74, 75, 76, 77, 78, 79
BIOSVersion            : ALASKA - 1072009, BIOS Date: 04/15/16 08:59:39 Ver:
04.06.05, BIOS Date: 04/15/16 08:59:39 Ver: 04.06.05
BuildNumber            :
Caption                : BIOS Date: 04/15/16 08:59:39 Ver: 04.06.05
CodeSet                :
CurrentLanguage        : en|US|iso8859-1
Description            : BIOS Date: 04/15/16 08:59:39 Ver: 04.06.05
IdentificationCode     :
InstallableLanguages   : 8
InstallDate            :
LanguageEdition        :
ListOfLanguages        : en|US|iso8859-1, fr|FR|iso8859-1, es|ES|i
so8859-1, de|DE|iso8859-1, ru|RU|iso8859-5, ja|JP|unicode, zh|TW|unicode,
zh|CN|unicode
Manufacturer           : American Megatrends Inc.
Name                   : BIOS Date: 04/15/16 08:59:39 Ver: 04.06.05
OtherTargetOS          :
PrimaryBIOS            : TRUE
ReleaseDate            : 04/15/2016 00:00:00
SerialNumber           : To be filled by O.E.M.
SMBIOSBIOSVersion      : 0901
SMBIOSMajorVersion     : 2
SMBIOSMinorVersion     : 7
SMBIOSPresent          : TRUE
SoftwareElementID      : BIOS Date: 04/15/16 08:59:39 Ver: 04.06.05
SoftwareElementState   : 3
Status                 : OK
TargetOperatingSystem: 0
Version                : ALASKA - 1072009
```

Going Back to the Future

Building an inventory of Namespaces and classes that are on your computer

HAVE TO BE THE FIRST TO ADMIT THAT THE SCRIPTS BELOW WEREN'T WRITTEN IN POWERSHELL. So, here's how this works. Create a directory folder on the desktop first and then Copy and Paste them there before running the scripts. Run the Namespaces first, then the categories second and the classes last. Give each about a minute head start.

Namespaces.VBS

```
Dim fso
Dim l
Dim s


EnumNamespaces("root")


Sub EnumNamespaces(ByVal nspace)

Set ws = createobject("Wscript.Shell")
Set fso = CreateObject("Scripting.FilesystemObject")

If fso.folderExists(ws.currentDirectory & "\" & nspace) = false then
 fso.CreateFolder(ws.currentDirectory & "\" & nspace)
End If
```

```vbscript
    On error Resume Next

    Set objs = GetObject("Winmgmts:\\.\" & nspace).InstancesOf("__Namespace", &H20000)

    If err.Number <> 0 Then
      err.Clear
      Exit Sub
    End If

    For each obj in objs

       EnumNamespaces(nspace & "\" & obj.Name)
    Next

    End Sub
```

Caregories.vbs

```vbscript
Dim fso
Dim l
Dim s

Set ws = createobject("Wscript.Shell")
Set fso = CreateObject("Scripting.FilesystemObject")

EnumNamespaces("root")


Sub EnumNamespaces(ByVal nspace)

EnumCategories(nspace)

If fso.folderExists(ws.currentDirectory & "\" & nspace) = false then
 fso.CreateFolder(ws.currentDirectory & "\" & nspace)
End If

On error Resume Next

Set objs = GetObject("Winmgmts:\\.\" & nspace).InstancesOf("__Namespace", &H20000)
```

```
If err.Number <> 0 Then
  err.Clear
  Exit Sub
End If

For each obj in objs

   EnumNamespaces(nspace & "\" & obj.Name)

Next

End Sub

Sub EnumCategories(ByVal nspace)

Set ws = createobject("Wscript.Shell")
Set fso = CreateObject("Scripting.FilesystemObject")

Set objs = GetObject("Winmgmts:\\.\" & nspace).SubClassesOf("", &H20000)
For each obj in objs

  pos = instr(obj.Path_.class, "_")

  if pos = 0 then
    If fso.folderExists(ws.currentDirectory & "\" & nspace & "\" & obj.Path_.Class) =
false then
       fso.CreateFolder(ws.currentDirectory & "\" & nspace & "\" & obj.Path_.Class)
    End If
  else
    if pos = 1 then
       If fso.folderExists(ws.currentDirectory & "\" & nspace & "\SuperClasses") =
false then
          fso.CreateFolder(ws.currentDirectory & "\" & nspace & "\SuperClasses")
       End If
    else
       If  fso.folderExists(ws.currentDirectory  &  "\"  &  nspace  &  "\"  &
Mid(obj.Path_.Class, 1, pos-1)) = false then
          fso.CreateFolder(ws.currentDirectory  &  "\"  &  nspace  &  "\"  &
Mid(obj.Path_.Class, 1, pos-1))
       End If
```

```
        End If
    End If

Next

End Sub
```

Classes.vbs

```vbs
Dim fso
Dim l
Dim s

EnumNamespaces("root")

Sub EnumNamespaces(ByVal nspace)

EnumClasses(nspace)

Set ws = createobject("Wscript.Shell")
Set fso = CreateObject("Scripting.FilesystemObject")

If fso.folderExists(ws.currentDirectory & "\" & nspace) = false then
 fso.CreateFolder(ws.currentDirectory & "\" & nspace)
End If

On error Resume Next

Set objs = GetObject("Winmgmts:\\.\" &    nspace).InstancesOf("___Namespace",
&H20000)

If err.Number <> 0 Then
 err.Clear
 Exit Sub
End If

For each obj in objs

    EnumNamespaces(nspace & "\" & obj.Name)
```

```
Next

End Sub

Sub EnumClasses(ByVal nspace)

Set ws = createobject("Wscript.Shell")
Set fso = CreateObject("Scripting.FilesystemObject")

Set objs = GetObject("Winmgmts:\\.\" & nspace).SubClassesOf("", &H20000)
For each obj in objs

   pos = instr(obj.Path_.class, "_")

  if pos = 0 then
     call CreateXMLFile(ws.CurrentDirectory & "\" & nspace & "\" & obj.Path_.Class,
nspace, obj.Path_.Class)
   else
     if pos = 1 then
        call CreateXMlFile(ws.CurrentDirectory & "\" & nspace & "\Superclasses",
nspace, obj.Path_.Class)
      else
        call CreateXMLFile(ws.CurrentDirectory & "\" & nspace & "\" &
Mid(obj.Path_.Class, 1, pos-1), nspace, obj.Path_.Class)
     End If
   End If

Next

End Sub

Sub CreateXMLFile(ByVal Path, ByVal nspace, ByVal ClassName)



Set fso = CreateObject("Scripting.FileSystemObject")
Dim shorty
On error Resume Next
shorty = fso.GetFolder(Path).ShortPath
```

```
If err.Number <> 0 then
err.Clear
Exit Sub
End IF


set obj = GetObject("Winmgmts:\\.\" &  nspace).Get(classname)

Set txtstream = fso.OpenTextFile(Shorty & "\" & Classname & ".xml", 2, true, -2)
txtstream.WriteLine("<data>")
txtstream.WriteLine("  <NamespaceInformation>")
txtstream.WriteLine("    <namespace>" & nspace & "</namespace>")
txtstream.WriteLine("    <classname>" & classname & "</classname>")
txtstream.WriteLine("  </NamespaceInformation>")
txtstream.WriteLine("  <properties>")

for each prop in obj.Properties_
    txtstream.WriteLine("    <property Name = """ & prop.Name & """ IsArray=""" &
prop.IsArray & """ DataType = """ & prop.Qualifiers_("CIMType").Value & """/>")
Next
txtstream.WriteLine("  </properties>")
txtstream.WriteLine("</data>")
txtstream.close

End sub
```

Once you give them a while to run, like ten minutes total, you should see this:

You could have more or you could have less. Either way, you probably have neve seen or thought there were that many classes before now.

May the power of WMI be with you!

Anyway, going to the root\CIMV2\Win32 folder, you will see the below files:

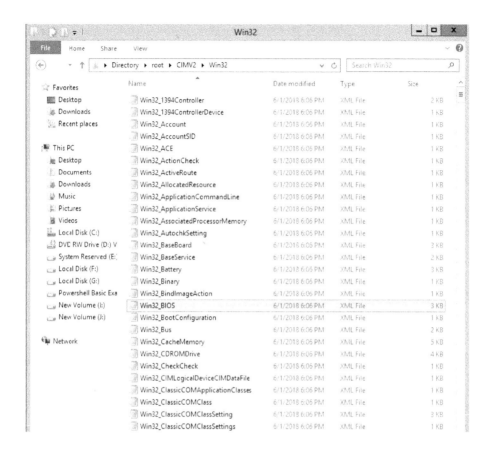

And the BIOS.xml looking like this:

Win32_BIOS - Notepad

File Edit Format View Help

```
<data>
  <NamespaceInformation>
    <namespace>root\CIMV2</namespace>
    <classname>Win32_BIOS</classname>
  </NamespaceInformation>
  <properties>
    <property Name = "BiosCharacteristics" IsArray="True" DataType = "uint16"/>
    <property Name = "BIOSVersion" IsArray="True" DataType = "string"/>
    <property Name = "BuildNumber" IsArray="False" DataType = "string"/>
    <property Name = "Caption" IsArray="False" DataType = "string"/>
    <property Name = "CodeSet" IsArray="False" DataType = "string"/>
    <property Name = "CurrentLanguage" IsArray="False" DataType = "string"/>
    <property Name = "Description" IsArray="False" DataType = "string"/>
    <property Name = "IdentificationCode" IsArray="False" DataType = "string"/>
    <property Name = "InstallableLanguages" IsArray="False" DataType = "uint16"/>
    <property Name = "InstallDate" IsArray="False" DataType = "datetime"/>
    <property Name = "LanguageEdition" IsArray="False" DataType = "string"/>
    <property Name = "ListOfLanguages" IsArray="True" DataType = "string"/>
    <property Name = "Manufacturer" IsArray="False" DataType = "string"/>
    <property Name = "Name" IsArray="False" DataType = "string"/>
    <property Name = "OtherTargetOS" IsArray="False" DataType = "string"/>
    <property Name = "PrimaryBIOS" IsArray="False" DataType = "boolean"/>
    <property Name = "ReleaseDate" IsArray="False" DataType = "datetime"/>
    <property Name = "SerialNumber" IsArray="False" DataType = "string"/>
    <property Name = "SMBIOSBIOSVersion" IsArray="False" DataType = "string"/>
    <property Name = "SMBIOSMajorVersion" IsArray="False" DataType = "uint16"/>
    <property Name = "SMBIOSMinorVersion" IsArray="False" DataType = "uint16"/>
    <property Name = "SMBIOSPresent" IsArray="False" DataType = "boolean"/>
    <property Name = "SoftwareElementID" IsArray="False" DataType = "string"/>
    <property Name = "SoftwareElementState" IsArray="False" DataType = "uint16"/>
    <property Name = "Status" IsArray="False" DataType = "string"/>
    <property Name = "TargetOperatingSystem" IsArray="False" DataType = "uint16"/>
    <property Name = "Version" IsArray="False" DataType = "string"/>
  </properties>
</data>
```

So, at this point we've profiled the classes and if we wanted to create programs from here without having to make WMI calls to pull up the need to know information to get the ball rolling.

Putting it all into motion

No time like now!

Okay, we are at that pivotal moment when we put all of this together so that we can accomplish something interesting. Let's work the arrays into the logic.

```
$Names
$Values

  function GetValue
  {
    param
    (
    [string]$Name,
    [object]$obj
    )
    [string]$PName = "`t" + $Name + " = "
    [string]$tempstr = $obj.GetText(0)
    $pos = $tempstr.IndexOf($PName)
    if ($pos -gt 0)
    {
      $pos = $pos + $PName.Length
      $tempstr = $tempstr.SubString($pos, ($tempstr.Length - $pos))
      $pos = $tempstr.IndexOf(";")
```

```
$tempstr = $tempstr.SubString(0, $pos)
$tempstr = $tempstr.Replace('"', "")
$tempstr = $tempstr.Replace("}", "")
$tempstr = $tempstr.Replace("{", "")
$tempstr = $tempstr.Trim()
if($tempstr.Length -gt 14)
{
  if($obj.Properties.Item($Name).Type -eq 101)
  {
   [System.String]$tstr = $tempstr.SubString(4, 2)
   $tstr = $tstr + "/"
   $tstr = $tstr + $tempstr.SubString(6, 2)
   $tstr = $tstr + "/"
   $tstr = $tstr + $tempstr.SubString(0, 4)
   $tstr = $tstr + " "
   $tstr = $tstr + $tempstr.SubString(8, 2)
   $tstr = $tstr + ":"
   $tstr = $tstr + $tempstr.SubString(10, 2)
   $tstr = $tstr + ":"
   $tstr = $tstr + $tempstr.SubString(12, 2)
   $tempstr = $tstr
  }
 }
 for($x=0;$x -lt $tempstr.Length; $x++)
 {
   if($tempstr[$x] -gt [char]120)
   {
       $tempstr[$x] -eq [char]32
   }
 }
 return $tempstr
}
else
{
 return ""
}
}

function WriteTheCode
{
```

```
param
(
[Array]$Names,
[Array]$Values
)

$tempstr = ""

$ws = new-object -com WScript.Shell
$fso = new-object -com Scripting.FileSystemObject
$txtstream = $fso.OpenTextFile($ws.CurrentDirectory + "\Process.csv", 2, $true, -
2)

for($x=0;$x -lt $Names.GetLength(0); $x++)
{
   if($tempstr -ne "")
   {
     $tempstr = $tempstr + ","
   }
   $tempstr = $tempstr + $Names[$x]
}
$txtstream.WriteLine($tempstr)
$tempstr = ""
for($y=0;$y -lt $Values.GetLength(0); $y++)
{
   for($x=0;$x -lt $Names.GetLength(0); $x++)
   {
      if($tempstr -ne "")
      {
        $tempstr = $tempstr + ","
      }
      $tempstr = $tempstr + '"' + $Values[$y, $x] + '"'
   }
   $txtstream.WriteLine($tempstr)
   $tempstr = ""
}
$txtstream.Close()
$ws.run($ws.CurrentDirectory + "\Process.csv")
```

```
}
$objs = GWMI -namespace root\cimv2 -class Win32_Process
if(! $objs.Count)
{
   $obj = $objs
   $Names=[Array]::CreateInstance([String], $obj.Properties.Count)
   $Value=[Array]::CreateInstance([String], 1, $obj.Properties.Count)

   $x = 0
   $y = 0

   foreach($prop in $obj.Properties)
   {
      $Names[$x] = $prop.Name
      $Values[0,$x] = GetValue $prop.Name $obj
      $x = $x + 1
   }
}
else
{

   foreach($obj in $objs)
   {
      $Names=[Array]::CreateInstance([String], $obj.Properties.Count)
      $Values=[Array]::CreateInstance([String], $objs.Count, $obj.Properties.Count)
      break
   }
   $x = 0
   $y = 0


   foreach($obj in $objs)
   {

      foreach($prop in $obj.Properties)
      {
         $Names[$x] = $prop.Name
         $x = $x + 1
      }
```

```
        break
    }
    $x = 0
    foreach($obj in $objs)
    {
        foreach($prop in $obj.Properties)
        {
            $Value = GetValue $prop.Name $obj
            $Values[$y, $x] = $Value
            $x = $x + 1
        }
        $x=0
        $y = $y + 1
    }

}

WriteTheCode $Names $Values
```

And this produces:

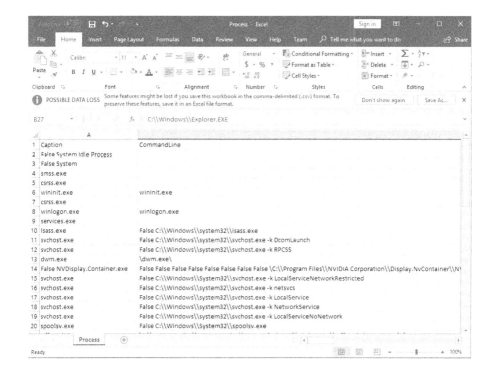

Of course, the code in the middle of the above routine can work on almost any kind of output

HTML with you in Mind
Reports and Tables and lots, lots more!

THE FIRST PARAGRAPH STYLE GIVES you nice spacing after the title, as well as the right indents for the first part of your text. Try adding uppercase letters to half of the first line for added styling. For even more stylistic impact, add a Drop Cap from the "Format…" menu in Microsoft Word. We recommend using a line height of three for the drop cap in this template.

```
$Names
$Values

    function GetValue
    {
      param
      (
      [string]$Name,
      [object]$obj
      )
      [string]$PName = "'`t" + $Name + " = "
      [string]$tempstr = $obj.GetText(0)
      $pos = $tempstr.IndexOf($PName)
      if ($pos -gt 0)
      {
        $pos = $pos + $PName.Length
        $tempstr = $tempstr.SubString($pos, ($tempstr.Length - $pos))
```

```
$pos = $tempstr.IndexOf(";")
$tempstr = $tempstr.SubString(0, $pos)
$tempstr = $tempstr.Replace("'", "")
$tempstr = $tempstr.Replace("}", "")
$tempstr = $tempstr.Replace("{", "")
$tempstr = $tempstr.Trim()
if($tempstr.Length -gt 14)
{
  if($obj.Propertics.Itcm($Name).Type -eq 101)
  {
    [System.String]$tstr = $tempstr.SubString(4, 2)
    $tstr = $tstr + "/"
    $tstr = $tstr + $tempstr.SubString(6, 2)
    $tstr = $tstr + "/"
    $tstr = $tstr + $tempstr.SubString(0, 4)
    $tstr = $tstr + " "
    $tstr = $tstr + $tempstr.SubString(8, 2)
    $tstr = $tstr + ":"
    $tstr = $tstr + $tempstr.SubString(10, 2)
    $tstr = $tstr + ":"
    $tstr = $tstr + $tempstr.SubString(12, 2)
    $tempstr = $tstr
  }
}
for($x=0;$x -lt $tempstr.Length; $x++)
{
  if($tempstr[$x] -gt [char]120)
  {
    $tempstr[$x] -eq [char]32
  }
}
return $tempstr
}
else
{
  return ""
}
}

function WriteTheHTMLCode
```

```
{
  param
  (
  [Array]$Names,
  [Array]$Values,
  [String]$Tablename,
  [String]$TableType,
  [String]$Orientation,
  [String]$ControlType
  )

  $tempstr = ""

  $ws = new-object -com WScript.Shell
  $fso = new-object -com Scripting.FileSystemObject
  $txtstream = $fso.OpenTextFile($ws.CurrentDirectory + "\" + $Tablename +
".html", 2, $true, -2)
  $txtstream.WriteLine("<html>")
  $txtstream.WriteLine("<head>")
  $txtstream.WriteLine("<title>" + $Tablename + "</title>")
  $txtstream.WriteLine("<body>")
  $txtstream.WriteLine("</br>")

  If($TableType -ne "Table")
  {
     $txtstream.WriteLine("<table border='0' cellspacing='3' cellpadding='3'>")
  }
  else
  {
     $txtstream.WriteLine("<table border='1' cellspacing='3' cellpadding='3'>")
  }
  if($Orientation -eq "Horizontal")
  {

     $txtstream.WriteLine("<tr>")
     for($x=0;$x -lt $Names.GetLength(0); $x++)
     {
        $txtstream.WriteLine("<th align='Left' nowrap style='font-family:Calibri,
Sans-Serif;font-size: 12px;color:darkred'>" + $Names[$x] + "</th>")
     }
```

```
    $txtstream.WriteLine("</tr>")

  for($y=0;$y -lt $Values.GetLength(0); $y++)
  {
     $txtstream.WriteLine("<tr>")
     for($x=0;$x -lt $Names.GetLength(0); $x++)
     {
        $tstr = $Values[$y,$x]
        switch($ControlType)
        {
           "None"{$txtstream.WriteLine("<td style='font-family:Calibri, Sans-
Serif;font-size:12px;color:navy;' align='left' nowrap='true'>" + $tstr +
"</td>")break}
           "Div" {$txtstream.WriteLine("<td style='font-family:Calibri, Sans-
Serif;font-size:12px;color:navy;' align='left' nowrap='true'><div>" + $tstr +
"</div></td>")break}
           "Span"{$txtstream.WriteLine("<td style='font-family:Calibri, Sans-
Serif;font-size:12px;color:navy;' align='left' nowrap='true'><span>" + $tstr +
"</span></td>")break}
           "Textarea"{$txtstream.WriteLine("<td style='font-family:Calibri, Sans-
Serif;font-size:12px;color:navy;' align='left' nowrap='true'><textarea>" + $tstr +
"</textarea></td>")break}
           "Textbox"{$txtstream.WriteLine("<td style='font-family:Calibri, Sans-
Serif;font-size:12px;color:navy;' align='left' nowrap='true'><input type=text
value="""" + $tstr + """"></input></td>")break}


        }

     }
     $txtstream.WriteLine("</tr>")
  }

}
else
{
   for($x=0;$x -lt $Names.GetLength(0); $x++)
   {
     $txtstream.WriteLine("<tr><th align='Left' nowrap style='font-family:Calibri,
Sans-Serif;font-size: 12px;color:darkred'>" + $Names[$x] + "</th>") break
     for($y=0;$y -lt $Values.GetLength(0); $y++)
```

```
        {
            $tstr = $Values[$y,$x]
            switch($ControlType)
            {

                "None"{$txtstream.WriteLine("<td style='font-family:Calibri, Sans-
Serif;font-size:12px;color:navy;' align='left' nowrap='true'>" + $tstr +
"</td>")break}
                "Div" {$txtstream.WriteLine("<td style='font-family:Calibri, Sans-
Serif;font-size:12px;color:navy;' align='left' nowrap='true'><div>" + $tstr +
"</div></td>")break}
                "Span"{$txtstream.WriteLine("<td style='font-family:Calibri, Sans-
Serif;font-size:12px;color:navy;' align='left' nowrap='true'><span>" + $tstr +
"</span></td>")break}
                "Textarea"{$txtstream.WriteLine("<td style='font-family:Calibri, Sans-
Serif;font-size:12px;color:navy;' align='left' nowrap='true'><textarea>" + $tstr +
"</textarea></td>")break}
                "Textbox"{$txtstream.WriteLine("<td align='left' nowrap='true'><input
style='font-family:Calibri, Sans-Serif;font-size:12px;color:navy;' type=text
value="""" + $tstr  + """"></input></td>")break}
            }

        }
        $txtstream.WriteLine("</tr>")
    }
}
$txtstream.WriteLine("</table>")
$txtstream.WriteLine("</body>")
$txtstream.WriteLine("</html>")
$txtstream.Close()

}


$objs = GWMI -namespace root\cimv2 -class Win32_Process
if(! $objs.Count)
{
    $obj = $objs
    $Names=[Array]::CreateInstance([String], $obj.Properties.Count)
    $Value=[Array]::CreateInstance([String], 1, $obj.Properties.Count)
```

```
   $x = 0
   $y = 0

   foreach($prop in $obj.Properties)
   {
     $Names[$x] = $prop.Name
     $Values[0,$x] = GetValue $prop.Name $obj
     $x = $x + 1
   }
}
else
{

   foreach($obj in $objs)
   {
     $Names=[Array]::CreateInstance([String], $obj.Properties.Count)
     $Values=[Array]::CreateInstance([String], $objs.Count, $obj.Properties.Count)
     break
   }
   $x = 0
   $y = 0


   foreach($obj in $objs)
   {

       foreach($prop in $obj.Properties)
       {
         $Names[$x] = $prop.Name
         $x = $x + 1
       }
       break
   }
   $x = 0
   foreach($obj in $objs)
   {
       foreach($prop in $obj.Properties)
       {
         $Value = GetValue $prop.Name $obj
```

```
        $Values[$y,$x] = $Value
        $x = $x + 1
    }
    $x=0
    $y = $y + 1
  }

}
```

WriteTheHTMLCode $Names $Values "Process" "Table" "Horizontal" "Textbox"

And this produces:

Caption	CommandLine	CreationClassName
False System Idle Proces		Win32_Process
False System		Win32_Process
smss.exe		Win32_Process
csrss.exe		Win32_Process
wininit.exe	wininit.exe	Win32_Process
csrss.exe		Win32_Process
winlogon.exe	winlogon.exe	Win32_Process
services.exe		Win32_Process
lsass.exe	False C:\\Windows\\syst	Win32_Process
svchost.exe	False C:\\Windows\\syst	Win32_Process
svchost.exe	False C:\\Windows\\syst	Win32_Process
dwm.exe	\dwm.exe\	Win32_Process

And the Vertical View:

Caption	System Idle Process	System
CommandLine		
CreationClassName	Win32_Process	Win32_Process
CreationDate		06/02/2018 01:09:33
CSCreationClassName	Win32_ComputerSystem	Win32_ComputerSystem
CSName	WIN-VNQ7KUKQ4NE	WIN-VNQ7KUKQ4NE
Description	System Idle Process	System
ExecutablePath		
ExecutionState		

Let's Do Some XML

From humble beginnings

W E CAN DO XML, AS WELL. I would like to show you a couple of examples doing it. Both of these examples have Database provider support and can also be used as ADO and OLEDB data sources.

Element XML

The idea here is to keep the code simple and supportive of what the providers can work with.

```
$Names
$Values

   function GetValue
   {
     param
     (
     [string]$Name,
     [object]$obj
     )
     [string]$PName = $Name + " = "
     [string]$tempstr = $obj.GetText(0)
     $pos = $tempstr.IndexOf($PName)
     if ($pos -gt 0)
```

```powershell
    {
      $pos = $pos + $PName.Length
      $tempstr = $tempstr.SubString($pos, ($tempstr.Length - $pos))
      $pos = $tempstr.IndexOf(";")
      $tempstr = $tempstr.SubString(0, $pos)
      $tempstr = $tempstr.Replace('"', "")
      $tempstr = $tempstr.Replace("}", "")
      $tempstr = $tempstr.Replace("{", "")
      $tempstr = $tempstr.Trim()
      if($tempstr.Length -gt 14)
      {
        if($obj.Properties.Item($Name).Type -eq 101)
        {
         [System.String]$tstr = $tempstr.SubString(4, 2)
         $tstr = $tstr + "/"
         $tstr = $tstr + $tempstr.SubString(6, 2)
         $tstr = $tstr + "/"
         $tstr = $tstr + $tempstr.SubString(0, 4)
         $tstr = $tstr + " "
         $tstr = $tstr + $tempstr.SubString(8, 2)
         $tstr = $tstr + ":"
         $tstr = $tstr + $tempstr.SubString(10, 2)
         $tstr = $tstr + ":"
         $tstr = $tstr + $tempstr.SubString(12, 2)
         $tempstr = $tstr
        }
      }
      return $tempstr
    }
    else
    {
      return ""
    }
  }

function WriteTheXMLCode
{
 param
 (
 [Array]$Names,
```

```powershell
    [Array]$Values,
    [String]$Tablename
    )

    $tempstr = ""

    $ws = new-object -com WScript.Shell
    $fso = new-object -com Scripting.FileSystemObject
    $txtstream = $fso.OpenTextFile($ws.CurrentDirectory + "\" + $Tablename +
".xml", 2, $true, -2)
    $txtstream.WriteLine("<?xml version='1.0' encoding='iso-8859-1'?>")
    $txtstream.WriteLine("<data>")
    for($y=0;$y -lt $Values.GetLength(0); $y++)
    {
        $txtstream.WriteLine("<" + $Tablename + ">")
        for($x=0;$x -lt $Names.GetLength(0); $x++)
        {
            $tstr = $Values[$y,$x]
            $txtstream.WriteLine("<" + $Names[$x] + ">" + $tstr + "</" +
$Names[$x] + ">")
        }
        $txtstream.WriteLine("</" + $Tablename + ">")
    }
    $txtstream.WriteLine("</data>")
    $txtstream.Close()
}


$objs = GWMI -namespace root\cimv2 -class Win32_Process
if(! $objs.Count)
{
    $obj = $objs
    $Names=[Array]::CreateInstance([String], $obj.Properties.Count)
    $Value=[Array]::CreateInstance([String], 1, $obj.Properties.Count)

    $x = 0
    $y = 0

    foreach($prop in $obj.Properties)
    {
```

```
            $Names[$x] = $prop.Name
            $Values[0,$x] = GetValue $prop.Name $obj
            $x = $x + 1
        }
    }
    else
    {

        foreach($obj in $objs)
        {
            $Names=[Array]::CreateInstance([String], $obj.Properties.Count)
            $Values=[Array]::CreateInstance([String], $objs.Count,
$obj.Properties.Count)
            break
        }
        $x = 0
        $y = 0


        foreach($obj in $objs)
        {

            foreach($prop in $obj.Properties)
            {
                $Names[$x] = $prop.Name
                $x = $x + 1
            }
            break
        }
        $x = 0
        foreach($obj in $objs)
        {
            foreach($prop in $obj.Properties)
            {
                $Value = GetValue $prop.Name $obj
                $Values[$y,$x] = $Value
                $x = $x + 1
            }
            $x=0
            $y = $y + 1
```

```
    }

}

WriteTheXMLCode $Names $Values "Process"
```

Here's what that looks like:

```xml
- <data>
  - <Process>
      <Caption>System Idle Process</Caption>
      <CommandLine/>
      <CreationClassName>Win32_Process</CreationClassName>
      <CreationDate/>
      <CSCreationClassName>Win32_ComputerSystem</CSCreationClassName>
      <CSName>WIN-VNQ7KUKQ4NE</CSName>
      <Description>System Idle Process</Description>
      <ExecutablePath/>
      <ExecutionState/>
      <Handle>0</Handle>
      <HandleCount>0</HandleCount>
      <InstallDate/>
      <KernelModeTime>1577399062500</KernelModeTime>
      <MaximumWorkingSetSize/>
      <MinimumWorkingSetSize/>
      <Name>Win32_Process</Name>
      <OSCreationClassName>Win32_OperatingSystem</OSCreationClassName>
    - <OSName>
        Microsoft Windows Server 2012 R2 Standard Evaluation|C:\\Windows|\\Device\\Harddisk1\\Partition2
      </OSName>
      <OtherOperationCount>0</OtherOperationCount>
      <OtherTransferCount>0</OtherTransferCount>
      <PageFaults>1</PageFaults>
      <PageFileUsage>0</PageFileUsage>
      <ParentProcessId>0</ParentProcessId>
      <PeakPageFileUsage>0</PeakPageFileUsage>
      <PeakVirtualSize>65536</PeakVirtualSize>
      <PeakWorkingSetSize>24</PeakWorkingSetSize>
      <Priority>0</Priority>
      <PrivatePageCount>0</PrivatePageCount>
      <ProcessId>0</ProcessId>
      <QuotaNonPagedPoolUsage>0</QuotaNonPagedPoolUsage>
      <QuotaPagedPoolUsage>0</QuotaPagedPoolUsage>
      <QuotaPeakNonPagedPoolUsage>0</QuotaPeakNonPagedPoolUsage>
      <QuotaPeakPagedPoolUsage>0</QuotaPeakPagedPoolUsage>
      <ReadOperationCount>0</ReadOperationCount>
      <ReadTransferCount>0</ReadTransferCount>
      <SessionId>0</SessionId>
      <Status/>
      <TerminationDate/>
      <ThreadCount>8</ThreadCount>
      <UserModeTime>0</UserModeTime>
      <VirtualSize>65536</VirtualSize>
      <WindowsVersion>6.3.9600</WindowsVersion>
      <WorkingSetSize>24</WorkingSetSize>
      <WriteOperationCount>0</WriteOperationCount>
      <WriteTransferCount>0</WriteTransferCount>
    </Process>
    -
```

Element XML For XSL

$Names
$Values

```
function GetValue
{
  param
  (
  [string]$Name,
  [object]$obj
  )
  [string]$PName = $Name + " = "
  [string]$tempstr = $obj.GetText(0)
  $pos = $tempstr.IndexOf($PName)
  if ($pos -gt 0)
  {
    $pos = $pos + $PName.Length
    $tempstr = $tempstr.SubString($pos, ($tempstr.Length - $pos))
    $pos = $tempstr.IndexOf(";")
    $tempstr = $tempstr.SubString(0, $pos)
    $tempstr = $tempstr.Replace("'", "")
    $tempstr = $tempstr.Replace("}", "")
    $tempstr = $tempstr.Replace("{", "")
    $tempstr = $tempstr.Trim()
    if($tempstr.Length -gt 14)
    {
      if($obj.Properties.Item($Name).Type -eq 101)
      {
        [System.String]$tstr = $tempstr.SubString(4, 2)
        $tstr = $tstr + "/"
        $tstr = $tstr + $tempstr.SubString(6, 2)
        $tstr = $tstr + "/"
        $tstr = $tstr + $tempstr.SubString(0, 4)
        $tstr = $tstr + " "
        $tstr = $tstr + $tempstr.SubString(8, 2)
        $tstr = $tstr + ":"
        $tstr = $tstr + $tempstr.SubString(10, 2)
        $tstr = $tstr + ":"
```

```
        $tstr = $tstr + $tempstr.SubString(12, 2)
        $tempstr = $tstr
      }
    }
    return $tempstr
  }
  else
  {
    return ""
  }
}

function WriteTheXMLCode
{
 param
 (
 [Array]$Names,
 [Array]$Values,
 [String]$Tablename
 )

 $tempstr = ""

 $ws = new-object -com WScript.Shell
 $fso = new-object -com Scripting.FileSystemObject
 $txtstream = $fso.OpenTextFile($ws.CurrentDirectory + "\" + $Tablename +
".xml", 2, $true, -2)
 $txtstream.WriteLine("<?xml version='1.0' encoding='iso-8859-1'?>")
 $txtstream.WriteLine("<?xml-stylesheet type='text/xsl' href='" + $Tablename +
".xsl'?>")
 $txtstream.WriteLine("<data>")
 for($y=0;$y -lt $Values.GetLength(0); $y++)
 {
    $txtstream.WriteLine("<" + $Tablename + ">")
    for($x=0;$x -lt $Names.GetLength(0); $x++)
    {
       $tstr = $Values[$y,$x]
       $txtstream.WriteLine("<" + $Names[$x] + ">" + $tstr + "</" + $Names[$x] +
">")
    }
```

```
     $txtstream.WriteLine("</" + $Tablename + ">")
 }
 $txtstream.WriteLine("</data>")
 $txtstream.Close()



}


$objs = GWMI -namespace root\cimv2 -class Win32_Process
if(! $objs.Count)
{
   $obj = $objs
   $Names=[Array]::CreateInstance([String], $obj.Properties.Count)
   $Value=[Array]::CreateInstance([String], 1, $obj.Properties.Count)

   $x = 0
   $y = 0

   foreach($prop in $obj.Properties)
   {
     $Names[$x] = $prop.Name
     $Values[0,$x] = GetValue $prop.Name $obj
     $x = $x + 1
   }
}
else
{

   foreach($obj in $objs)
   {
     $Names=[Array]::CreateInstance([String], $obj.Properties.Count)
     $Values=[Array]::CreateInstance([String], $objs.Count, $obj.Properties.Count)
     break
   }
   $x = 0
   $y = 0
```

```
    foreach($obj in $objs)
    {

        foreach($prop in $obj.Properties)
        {
            $Names[$x] = $prop.Name
            $x = $x + 1
        }
        break
    }
    $x = 0
    foreach($obj in $objs)
    {
        foreach($prop in $obj.Properties)
        {
            $Value = GetValue $prop.Name $obj
            $Values[$y,$x] = $Value
            $x = $x + 1
        }
        $x=0
        $y = $y + 1
    }

}

WriteTheXMLCode $Names $Values "Process"
```

Schema.XML

```
$Names
$Values

    function GetValue
    {
        param
        (
        [string]$Name,
```

```powershell
  [object]$obj
  )
  [string]$PName = $Name + " = "
  [string]$tempstr = $obj.GetText(0)
  $pos = $tempstr.IndexOf($PName)
  if ($pos -gt 0)
  {
    $pos = $pos + $PName.Length
    $tempstr = $tempstr.SubString($pos, ($tempstr.Length - $pos))
    $pos = $tempstr.IndexOf(";")
    $tempstr = $tempstr.SubString(0, $pos)
    $tempstr = $tempstr.Replace('"', "")
    $tempstr = $tempstr.Replace("}", "")
    $tempstr = $tempstr.Replace("{", "")
    $tempstr = $tempstr.Trim()
    if($tempstr.Length -gt 14)
    {
      if($obj.Properties.Item($Name).Type -eq 101)
      {
        [System.String]$tstr = $tempstr.SubString(4, 2)
        $tstr = $tstr + "/"
        $tstr = $tstr + $tempstr.SubString(6, 2)
        $tstr = $tstr + "/"
        $tstr = $tstr + $tempstr.SubString(0, 4)
        $tstr = $tstr + " "
        $tstr = $tstr + $tempstr.SubString(8, 2)
        $tstr = $tstr + ":"
        $tstr = $tstr + $tempstr.SubString(10, 2)
        $tstr = $tstr + ":"
        $tstr = $tstr + $tempstr.SubString(12, 2)
        $tempstr = $tstr
      }
    }
    return $tempstr
  }
  else
  {
    return ""
  }
}
```

```
function WriteTheXMLCode
{
 param
 (
 [Array]$Names,
 [Array]$Values,
 [String]$Tablename
 )

 $tempstr = ""

 $ws = new-object -com WScript.Shell
 $fso = new-object -com Scripting.FileSystemObject
 $txtstream = $fso.OpenTextFile($ws.CurrentDirectory + "\" + $Tablename   +
".xml", 2, $true, -2)
 $txtstream.WriteLine("<?xml version='1.0' encoding='iso-8859-1'?>")
 $txtstream.WriteLine("<data>")
 for($y=0;$y -lt $Values.GetLength(0); $y++)
 {
    $txtstream.WriteLine("<" + $Tablename + ">")
    for($x=0;$x -lt $Names.GetLength(0); $x++)
    {
      $tstr = $Values[$y,$x]
      $txtstream.WriteLine("<" + $Names[$x] + ">" + $tstr + "</" + $Names[$x] +
">")
    }
    $txtstream.WriteLine("</" + $Tablename + ">")
 }
 $txtstream.WriteLine("</data>")
 $txtstream.Close()

 $cn = new-object -com ADODB.Connection
 $cn.ConnectionString = "Provider=MSDAOSP;Data Source=Msxml2.DSOControl"
 $cn.Open()

 $rs = new-object -com ADODB.Recordset
 $rs.ActiveConnection = $cn
 $rs.Open($ws.CurrentDirectory + "\" + $Tablename  + ".xml")
 $rs.Save($ws.CurrentDirectory + "\" + $Tablename  + "Schema.xml", 1)
```

```
}


$objs = GWMI -namespace root\cimv2 -class Win32_Process
if(! $objs.Count)
{
   $obj = $objs
   $Names=[Array]::CreateInstance([String], $obj.Properties.Count)
   $Value=[Array]::CreateInstance([String], 1, $obj.Properties.Count)

   $x = 0
   $y = 0

   foreach($prop in $obj.Properties)
   {
      $Names[$x] = $prop.Name
      $Values[0,$x] = GetValue $prop.Name $obj
      $x = $x + 1
   }
}
else
{

   foreach($obj in $objs)
   {
      $Names=[Array]::CreateInstance([String], $obj.Properties.Count)
      $Values=[Array]::CreateInstance([String], $objs.Count, $obj.Properties.Count)
      break
   }
   $x = 0
   $y = 0


   foreach($obj in $objs)
   {

      foreach($prop in $obj.Properties)
      {
         $Names[$x] = $prop.Name
```

```
            $x = $x + 1
        }
        break
    }
    $x = 0
    foreach($obj in $objs)
    {
        foreach($prop in $obj.Properties)
        {
            $Value = GetValue $prop.Name $obj
            $Values[$y,$x] = $Value
            $x = $x + 1
        }
        $x=0
        $y = $y + 1
    }

}

WriteTheXMLCode $Names $Values "Process"
```

XSL
The logical choice

T SEEMS LOGICAL, SINCE I JUST SHOWED YOU HOW TO CREATE ELEMENT XML FOR XSL, TO INCLUDE A ROUTINE THAT PRODUCES XSL. There are four ways to do the rendering and all work to get the job done.

Single Line Horizontal

```
$Names
$Values

   function GetValue
   {
     param
     (
     [string]$Name,
     [object]$obj
     )
     [string]$PName = $Name + " = "
     [string]$tempstr = $obj.GetText(0)
     $pos = $tempstr.IndexOf($PName)
     if ($pos -gt 0)
     {
       $pos = $pos + $PName.Length
       $tempstr = $tempstr.SubString($pos, ($tempstr.Length - $pos))
       $pos = $tempstr.IndexOf(";")
```

```
        $tempstr = $tempstr.SubString(0, $pos)
        $tempstr = $tempstr.Replace("'", "")
        $tempstr = $tempstr.Replace("}", "")
        $tempstr = $tempstr.Replace("{", "")
        $tempstr = $tempstr.Trim()
        if($tempstr.Length -gt 14)
        {
         if($obj.Properties.Item($Name).Type -eq 101)
          {
           [System.String]$tstr = $tempstr.SubString(4, 2)
           $tstr = $tstr + "/"
           $tstr = $tstr + $tempstr.SubString(6, 2)
           $tstr = $tstr + "/"
           $tstr = $tstr + $tempstr.SubString(0, 4)
           $tstr = $tstr + " "
           $tstr = $tstr + $tempstr.SubString(8, 2)
           $tstr = $tstr + ":"
           $tstr = $tstr + $tempstr.SubString(10, 2)
           $tstr = $tstr + ":"
           $tstr = $tstr + $tempstr.SubString(12, 2)
           $tempstr = $tstr
          }
         }
         return $tempstr
        }
        else
        {
         return ""
        }
   }

function WriteTheXSLCode
{
 param
 (
 [Array]$Names,
 [Array]$Values,
 [String]$Tablename
 )
```

```
$tempstr = ""

$ws = new-object -com WScript.Shell
$fso = new-object -com Scripting.FileSystemObject
$txtstream = $fso.OpenTextFile($ws.CurrentDirectory + "\" + $Tablename +
".xsl", 2, $true, -2)
$txtstream.WriteLine("<?xml version='1.0' encoding='iso-8859-1'?>")
$txtstream.WriteLine("<xsl:stylesheet                              version='1.0'
xmlns:xsl='http://www.w3.org/1999/XSL/Transform'>")
$txtstream.WriteLine("<xsl:template match=""/"">")
$txtstream.WriteLine("<html>")
$txtstream.WriteLine("<head>")
$txtstream.WriteLine("<title>Products</title>")
$txtstream.WriteLine("<style type='text/css'>")
$txtstream.WriteLine("th")
$txtstream.WriteLine("{")
$txtstream.WriteLine("   COLOR: black;")
$txtstream.WriteLine("   BACKGROUND-COLOR: white;")
$txtstream.WriteLine("   FONT-FAMILY:font-family: Cambria, serif;")
$txtstream.WriteLine("   FONT-SIZE: 12px;")
$txtstream.WriteLine("   text-align: left;")
$txtstream.WriteLine("   white-Space: nowrap;")
$txtstream.WriteLine("}")
$txtstream.WriteLine("td")
$txtstream.WriteLine("{")
$txtstream.WriteLine("   COLOR: black;")
$txtstream.WriteLine("   BACKGROUND-COLOR: white;")
$txtstream.WriteLine("   FONT-FAMILY: font-family: Cambria, serif;")
$txtstream.WriteLine("   FONT-SIZE: 12px;")
$txtstream.WriteLine("   text-align: left;")
$txtstream.WriteLine("   white-Space: nowrap;")
$txtstream.WriteLine("}")
$txtstream.WriteLine("div")
$txtstream.WriteLine("{")
$txtstream.WriteLine("   COLOR: black;")
$txtstream.WriteLine("   BACKGROUND-COLOR: white;")
$txtstream.WriteLine("   FONT-FAMILY: font-family: Cambria, serif;")
$txtstream.WriteLine("   FONT-SIZE: 10px;")
$txtstream.WriteLine("   text-align: left;")
$txtstream.WriteLine("   white-Space: nowrap;")
```

```
$txtstream.WriteLine("}")
$txtstream.WriteLine("span")
$txtstream.WriteLine("{")
$txtstream.WriteLine("    COLOR: black;")
$txtstream.WriteLine("    BACKGROUND-COLOR: white;")
$txtstream.WriteLine("    FONT-FAMILY: font-family: Cambria, serif;")
$txtstream.WriteLine("    FONT-SIZE: 10px;")
$txtstream.WriteLine("    text-align: left;")
$txtstream.WriteLine("    white-Space: nowrap;")
$txtstream.WriteLine("    display:inline-block;")
$txtstream.WriteLine("    width: 100%;")
$txtstream.WriteLine("}")
$txtstream.WriteLine("textarea")
$txtstream.WriteLine("{")
$txtstream.WriteLine("    COLOR: black;")
$txtstream.WriteLine("    BACKGROUND-COLOR: white;")
$txtstream.WriteLine("    FONT-FAMILY: font-family: Cambria, serif;")
$txtstream.WriteLine("    FONT-SIZE: 10px;")
$txtstream.WriteLine("    text-align: left;")
$txtstream.WriteLine("    white-Space: nowrap;")
$txtstream.WriteLine("    width: 100%;")
$txtstream.WriteLine("}")
$txtstream.WriteLine("select")
$txtstream.WriteLine("{")
$txtstream.WriteLine("    COLOR: black;")
$txtstream.WriteLine("    BACKGROUND-COLOR: white;")
$txtstream.WriteLine("    FONT-FAMILY: font-family: Cambria, serif;")
$txtstream.WriteLine("    FONT-SIZE: 10px;")
$txtstream.WriteLine("    text-align: left;")
$txtstream.WriteLine("    white-Space: nowrap;")
$txtstream.WriteLine("    width: 100%;")
$txtstream.WriteLine("}")
$txtstream.WriteLine("input")
$txtstream.WriteLine("{")
$txtstream.WriteLine("    COLOR: black;")
$txtstream.WriteLine("    BACKGROUND-COLOR: white;")
$txtstream.WriteLine("    FONT-FAMILY: font-family: Cambria, serif;")
$txtstream.WriteLine("    FONT-SIZE: 12px;")
$txtstream.WriteLine("    text-align: left;")
$txtstream.WriteLine("    display:table-cell;")
```

```
$txtstream.WriteLine("    white-Space: nowrap;")
$txtstream.WriteLine("}")
$txtstream.WriteLine("h1 {")
$txtstream.WriteLine("color: antiquewhite;")
$txtstream.WriteLine("text-shadow: 1px 1px 1px black;")
$txtstream.WriteLine("padding: 3px;")
$txtstream.WriteLine("text-align: center;")
$txtstream.WriteLine("box-shadow: invar 2px 2px 5px rgba(0,0,0,0.5), invar -
2px -2px 5px rgba(255,255,255,0.5);")
$txtstream.WriteLine("}")
$txtstream.WriteLine("</style>")
$txtstream.WriteLine("</head>")
$txtstream.WriteLine("<body>")
$txtstream.WriteLine("<table           border=""0""          Cellpadding=""2""
cellspacing=""2"">")
$txtstream.WriteLine("<tr>")
for($x=0;$x -lt $Names.GetLength(0); $x++)
{
    $txtstream.WriteLine("<th>" + $Names[$x] + "</th>")
}
$txtstream.WriteLine("</tr>")
 $txtstream.WriteLine("<tr>")
for($x=0;$x -lt $Names.GetLength(0); $x++)
{
    $txtstream.WriteLine("<td         align='left'    nowrap='true'><xsl:value-of
select="" data/" + $Tablename + "/" + $Names[$x]  + """/></td>")
}
$txtstream.WriteLine("</tr>")
$txtstream.WriteLine("</table>")
$txtstream.WriteLine("</body>")
$txtstream.WriteLine("</html>")
$txtstream.WriteLine("</xsl:template>")
$txtstream.WriteLine("</xsl:stylesheet>")
$txtstream.Close()

}


$objs = GWMI -namespace root\cimv2 -class Win32_Process
if(! $objs.Count)
```

```
{
    $obj = $objs
    $Names=[Array]::CreateInstance([String], $obj.Properties.Count)
    $Value=[Array]::CreateInstance([String], 1, $obj.Properties.Count)

    $x = 0
    $y = 0

    foreach($prop in $obj.Properties)
    {
        $Names[$x] = $prop.Name
        $Values[0,$x] = GetValue $prop.Name $obj
        $x = $x + 1
    }
}
else
{

    foreach($obj in $objs)
    {
        $Names=[Array]::CreateInstance([String], $obj.Properties.Count)
        $Values=[Array]::CreateInstance([String],                    $objs.Count,
$obj.Properties.Count)
        break
    }
    $x = 0
    $y = 0


    foreach($obj in $objs)
    {

        foreach($prop in $obj.Properties)
        {
            $Names[$x] = $prop.Name
            $x = $x + 1
        }
        break
    }
    $x = 0
```

```
    foreach($obj in $objs)
    {
        foreach($prop in $obj.Properties)
        {
            $Value = GetValue $prop.Name $obj
            $Values[$y,$x] = $Value
            $x = $x + 1
        }
        $x=0
        $y = $y + 1
    }


}

WriteTheXSLCode $Names $Values "Process"
```

Multi-Line Horizontal

```
$Names
$Values

    function GetValue
    {
        param
        (
        [string]$Name,
        [object]$obj
        )
        [string]$PName = $Name + " = "
        [string]$tempstr = $obj.GetText(0)
        $pos = $tempstr.IndexOf($PName)
        if ($pos -gt 0)
        {
          $pos = $pos + $PName.Length
          $tempstr = $tempstr.SubString($pos, ($tempstr.Length - $pos))
          $pos = $tempstr.IndexOf(";")
          $tempstr = $tempstr.SubString(0, $pos)
```

```
      $tempstr = $tempstr.Replace("'", "")
      $tempstr = $tempstr.Replace("}", "")
      $tempstr = $tempstr.Replace("{", "")
      $tempstr = $tempstr.Trim()
      if($tempstr.Length -gt 14)
      {
        if($obj.Properties.Item($Name).Type -eq 101)
        {
          [System.String]$tstr = $tempstr.SubString(4, 2)
          $tstr = $tstr + "/"
          $tstr = $tstr + $tempstr.SubString(6, 2)
          $tstr = $tstr + "/"
          $tstr = $tstr + $tempstr.SubString(0, 4)
          $tstr = $tstr + " "
          $tstr = $tstr + $tempstr.SubString(8, 2)
          $tstr = $tstr + ":"
          $tstr = $tstr + $tempstr.SubString(10, 2)
          $tstr = $tstr + ":"
          $tstr = $tstr + $tempstr.SubString(12, 2)
          $tempstr = $tstr
        }
      }
      return $tempstr
    }
    else
    {
      return ""
    }
  }

function WriteTheXSLCode
{
 param
 (
 [Array]$Names,
 [Array]$Values,
 [String]$Tablename
 )

 $tempstr = ""
```

```
$ws = new-object -com WScript.Shell
$fso = new-object -com Scripting.FileSystemObject
$txtstream = $fso.OpenTextFile($ws.CurrentDirectory + "\" + $Tablename + ".xsl", 2, $true, -2)
$txtstream.WriteLine("<?xml version='1.0' encoding='iso-8859-1'?>")
$txtstream.WriteLine("<xsl:stylesheet                    version='1.0' xmlns:xsl='http://www.w3.org/1999/XSL/Transform'>")
$txtstream.WriteLine("<xsl:template match=""/"">")
$txtstream.WriteLine("<html>")
$txtstream.WriteLine("<head>")
$txtstream.WriteLine("<title>Products</title>")
$txtstream.WriteLine("<style type='text/css'>")
$txtstream.WriteLine("th")
$txtstream.WriteLine("{")
$txtstream.WriteLine("   COLOR: black;")
$txtstream.WriteLine("   BACKGROUND-COLOR: white;")
$txtstream.WriteLine("   FONT-FAMILY:font-family: Cambria, serif;")
$txtstream.WriteLine("   FONT-SIZE: 12px;")
$txtstream.WriteLine("   text-align: left;")
$txtstream.WriteLine("   white-Space: nowrap;")
$txtstream.WriteLine("}")
$txtstream.WriteLine("td")
$txtstream.WriteLine("{")
$txtstream.WriteLine("   COLOR: black;")
$txtstream.WriteLine("   BACKGROUND-COLOR: white;")
$txtstream.WriteLine("   FONT-FAMILY: font-family: Cambria, serif;")
$txtstream.WriteLine("   FONT-SIZE: 12px;")
$txtstream.WriteLine("   text-align: left;")
$txtstream.WriteLine("   white-Space: nowrap;")
$txtstream.WriteLine("}")
$txtstream.WriteLine("div")
$txtstream.WriteLine("{")
$txtstream.WriteLine("   COLOR: black;")
$txtstream.WriteLine("   BACKGROUND-COLOR: white;")
$txtstream.WriteLine("   FONT-FAMILY: font-family: Cambria, serif;")
$txtstream.WriteLine("   FONT-SIZE: 10px;")
$txtstream.WriteLine("   text-align: left;")
$txtstream.WriteLine("   white-Space: nowrap;")
$txtstream.WriteLine("}")
```

```
$txtstream.WriteLine("span")
$txtstream.WriteLine("{")
$txtstream.WriteLine("    COLOR: black;")
$txtstream.WriteLine("    BACKGROUND-COLOR: white;")
$txtstream.WriteLine("    FONT-FAMILY: font-family: Cambria, serif;")
$txtstream.WriteLine("    FONT-SIZE: 10px;")
$txtstream.WriteLine("    text-align: left;")
$txtstream.WriteLine("    white-Space: nowrap;")
$txtstream.WriteLine("    display:inline-block;")
$txtstream.WriteLine("    width: 100%;")
$txtstream.WriteLine("}")
$txtstream.WriteLine("textarea")
$txtstream.WriteLine("{")
$txtstream.WriteLine("    COLOR: black;")
$txtstream.WriteLine("    BACKGROUND-COLOR: white;")
$txtstream.WriteLine("    FONT-FAMILY: font-family: Cambria, serif;")
$txtstream.WriteLine("    FONT-SIZE: 10px;")
$txtstream.WriteLine("    text-align: left;")
$txtstream.WriteLine("    white-Space: nowrap;")
$txtstream.WriteLine("    width: 100%;")
$txtstream.WriteLine("}")
$txtstream.WriteLine("select")
$txtstream.WriteLine("{")
$txtstream.WriteLine("    COLOR: black;")
$txtstream.WriteLine("    BACKGROUND-COLOR: white;")
$txtstream.WriteLine("    FONT-FAMILY: font-family: Cambria, serif;")
$txtstream.WriteLine("    FONT-SIZE: 10px;")
$txtstream.WriteLine("    text-align: left;")
$txtstream.WriteLine("    white-Space: nowrap;")
$txtstream.WriteLine("    width: 100%;")
$txtstream.WriteLine("}")
$txtstream.WriteLine("input")
$txtstream.WriteLine("{")
$txtstream.WriteLine("    COLOR: black;")
$txtstream.WriteLine("    BACKGROUND-COLOR: white;")
$txtstream.WriteLine("    FONT-FAMILY: font-family: Cambria, serif;")
$txtstream.WriteLine("    FONT-SIZE: 12px;")
$txtstream.WriteLine("    text-align: left;")
$txtstream.WriteLine("    display:table-cell;")
$txtstream.WriteLine("    white-Space: nowrap;")
```

```powershell
$txtstream.WriteLine("}")
$txtstream.WriteLine("h1 {")
$txtstream.WriteLine("color: antiquewhite;")
$txtstream.WriteLine("text-shadow: 1px 1px 1px black;")
$txtstream.WriteLine("padding: 3px;")
$txtstream.WriteLine("text-align: center;")
$txtstream.WriteLine("box-shadow: invar 2px 2px 5px rgba(0,0,0,0.5), invar -2px -2px 5px rgba(255,255,255,0.5);")
$txtstream.WriteLine("}")
$txtstream.WriteLine("</style>")
$txtstream.WriteLine("</head>")
$txtstream.WriteLine("<body>")
$txtstream.WriteLine("<table          border=""0""          Cellpadding=""2"" cellspacing=""2"">")
$txtstream.WriteLine("<tr>")
for($x=0;$x -lt $Names.GetLength(0); $x++)
{
    $txtstream.WriteLine("<th>" + $Names[$x] + "</th>")
}
$txtstream.WriteLine("</tr>")
$txtstream.WriteLine("<xsl:for-each select=""data/" + $Tablename + """>")
$txtstream.WriteLine("<tr>")
for($x=0;$x -lt $Names.GetLength(0); $x++)
{
    $txtstream.WriteLine("<td          align='left'     nowrap='true'><xsl:value-of select=""" + $Names[$x]  + """/></td>")
}
$txtstream.WriteLine("</tr>")
$txtstream.WriteLine("</xsl:for-each>")
$txtstream.WriteLine("</table>")
$txtstream.WriteLine("</body>")
$txtstream.WriteLine("</html>")
$txtstream.WriteLine("</xsl:template>")
$txtstream.WriteLine("</xsl:stylesheet>")
$txtstream.Close()

}


$objs = GWMI -namespace root\cimv2 -class Win32_Process
```

```
if(! $objs.Count)
{
   $obj = $objs
   $Names=[Array]::CreateInstance([String], $obj.Properties.Count)
   $Value=[Array]::CreateInstance([String], 1, $obj.Properties.Count)

   $x = 0
   $y = 0

   foreach($prop in $obj.Properties)
   {
      $Names[$x] = $prop.Name
      $Values[0,$x] = GetValue $prop.Name $obj
      $x = $x + 1
   }
}
else
{

   foreach($obj in $objs)
   {
      $Names=[Array]::CreateInstance([String], $obj.Properties.Count)
      $Values=[Array]::CreateInstance([String],                    $objs.Count,
$obj.Properties.Count)
      break
   }
   $x = 0
   $y = 0


   foreach($obj in $objs)
   {

      foreach($prop in $obj.Properties)
      {
         $Names[$x] = $prop.Name
         $x = $x + 1
      }
      break
   }
```

```
    $x = 0
    foreach($obj in $objs)
    {
        foreach($prop in $obj.Properties)
        {
            $Value = GetValue $prop.Name $obj
            $Values[$y,$x] = $Value
            $x = $x + 1
        }
        $x=0
        $y = $y + 1
    }

}

WriteTheXSLCode $Names $Values "Process"
```

Single Line Vertical

```
$Names
$Values

    function GetValue
    {
      param
      (
      [string]$Name,
      [object]$obj
      )
      [string]$PName = $Name + " = "
      [string]$tempstr = $obj.GetText(0)
      $pos = $tempstr.IndexOf($PName)
      if ($pos -gt 0)
      {
        $pos = $pos + $PName.Length
        $tempstr = $tempstr.SubString($pos, ($tempstr.Length - $pos))
        $pos = $tempstr.IndexOf(";")
        $tempstr = $tempstr.SubString(0, $pos)
```

```
      $tempstr = $tempstr.Replace("'", "")
      $tempstr = $tempstr.Replace("}", "")
      $tempstr = $tempstr.Replace("{", "")
      $tempstr = $tempstr.Trim()
      if($tempstr.Length -gt 14)
      {
       if($obj.Properties.Item($Name).Type -eq 101)
        {
         [System.String]$tstr = $tempstr.SubString(4, 2)
         $tstr = $tstr + "/"
         $tstr = $tstr + $tempstr.SubString(6, 2)
         $tstr = $tstr + "/"
         $tstr = $tstr + $tempstr.SubString(0, 4)
         $tstr = $tstr + " "
         $tstr = $tstr + $tempstr.SubString(8, 2)
         $tstr = $tstr + ":"
         $tstr = $tstr + $tempstr.SubString(10, 2)
         $tstr = $tstr + ":"
         $tstr = $tstr + $tempstr.SubString(12, 2)
         $tempstr = $tstr
        }
       }
       return $tempstr
      }
      else
      {
       return ""
      }
   }

function WriteTheXSLCode
{
 param
 (
 [Array]$Names,
 [Array]$Values,
 [String]$Tablename
 )

 $tempstr = ""
```

```
$ws = new-object -com WScript.Shell
$fso = new-object -com Scripting.FileSystemObject
$txtstream = $fso.OpenTextFile($ws.CurrentDirectory + "\" + $Tablename + ".xsl", 2, $true, -2)
$txtstream.WriteLine("<?xml version='1.0' encoding='iso-8859-1'?>")
$txtstream.WriteLine("<xsl:stylesheet                    version='1.0' xmlns:xsl='http://www.w3.org/1999/XSL/Transform'>")
$txtstream.WriteLine("<xsl:template match=""""/"""">")
$txtstream.WriteLine("<html>")
$txtstream.WriteLine("<head>")
$txtstream.WriteLine("<title>Products</title>")
$txtstream.WriteLine("<style type='text/css'>")
$txtstream.WriteLine("th")
$txtstream.WriteLine("{")
$txtstream.WriteLine("    COLOR: black;")
$txtstream.WriteLine("    BACKGROUND-COLOR: white;")
$txtstream.WriteLine("    FONT-FAMILY:font-family: Cambria, serif;")
$txtstream.WriteLine("    FONT-SIZE: 12px;")
$txtstream.WriteLine("    text-align: left;")
$txtstream.WriteLine("    white-Space: nowrap;")
$txtstream.WriteLine("}")
$txtstream.WriteLine("td")
$txtstream.WriteLine("{")
$txtstream.WriteLine("    COLOR: black;")
$txtstream.WriteLine("    BACKGROUND-COLOR: white;")
$txtstream.WriteLine("    FONT-FAMILY: font-family: Cambria, serif;")
$txtstream.WriteLine("    FONT-SIZE: 12px;")
$txtstream.WriteLine("    text-align: left;")
$txtstream.WriteLine("    white-Space: nowrap;")
$txtstream.WriteLine("}")
$txtstream.WriteLine("div")
$txtstream.WriteLine("{")
$txtstream.WriteLine("    COLOR: black;")
$txtstream.WriteLine("    BACKGROUND-COLOR: white;")
$txtstream.WriteLine("    FONT-FAMILY: font-family: Cambria, serif;")
$txtstream.WriteLine("    FONT-SIZE: 10px;")
$txtstream.WriteLine("    text-align: left;")
$txtstream.WriteLine("    white-Space: nowrap;")
$txtstream.WriteLine("}")
```

```
$txtstream.WriteLine("span")
$txtstream.WriteLine("{")
$txtstream.WriteLine("    COLOR: black;")
$txtstream.WriteLine("    BACKGROUND-COLOR: white;")
$txtstream.WriteLine("    FONT-FAMILY: font-family: Cambria, serif;")
$txtstream.WriteLine("    FONT-SIZE: 10px;")
$txtstream.WriteLine("    text-align: left;")
$txtstream.WriteLine("    white-Space: nowrap;")
$txtstream.WriteLine("    display:inline-block;")
$txtstream.WriteLine("    width: 100%;")
$txtstream.WriteLine("}")
$txtstream.WriteLine("textarea")
$txtstream.WriteLine("{")
$txtstream.WriteLine("    COLOR: black;")
$txtstream.WriteLine("    BACKGROUND-COLOR: white;")
$txtstream.WriteLine("    FONT-FAMILY: font-family: Cambria, serif;")
$txtstream.WriteLine("    FONT-SIZE: 10px;")
$txtstream.WriteLine("    text-align: left;")
$txtstream.WriteLine("    white-Space: nowrap;")
$txtstream.WriteLine("    width: 100%;")
$txtstream.WriteLine("}")
$txtstream.WriteLine("select")
$txtstream.WriteLine("{")
$txtstream.WriteLine("    COLOR: black;")
$txtstream.WriteLine("    BACKGROUND-COLOR: white;")
$txtstream.WriteLine("    FONT-FAMILY: font-family: Cambria, serif;")
$txtstream.WriteLine("    FONT-SIZE: 10px;")
$txtstream.WriteLine("    text-align: left;")
$txtstream.WriteLine("    white-Space: nowrap;")
$txtstream.WriteLine("    width: 100%;")
$txtstream.WriteLine("}")
$txtstream.WriteLine("input")
$txtstream.WriteLine("{")
$txtstream.WriteLine("    COLOR: black;")
$txtstream.WriteLine("    BACKGROUND-COLOR: white;")
$txtstream.WriteLine("    FONT-FAMILY: font-family: Cambria, serif;")
$txtstream.WriteLine("    FONT-SIZE: 12px;")
$txtstream.WriteLine("    text-align: left;")
$txtstream.WriteLine("    display:table-cell;")
$txtstream.WriteLine("    white-Space: nowrap;")
```

```
$txtstream.WriteLine("}")
$txtstream.WriteLine("h1 {")
$txtstream.WriteLine("color: antiquewhite;")
$txtstream.WriteLine("text-shadow: 1px 1px 1px black;")
$txtstream.WriteLine("padding: 3px;")
$txtstream.WriteLine("text-align: center;")
$txtstream.WriteLine("box-shadow: invar 2px 2px 5px rgba(0,0,0,0.5), invar -
2px -2px 5px rgba(255,255,255,0.5);")
$txtstream.WriteLine("}")
$txtstream.WriteLine("</style>")
$txtstream.WriteLine("</head>")
$txtstream.WriteLine("<body>")
$txtstream.WriteLine("<table           border=""0""        Cellpadding=""2""
cellspacing=""2"">")
$txtstream.WriteLine("<tr>")
for($x=0;$x -lt $Names.GetLength(0); $x++)
{
    $txtstream.WriteLine("<tr><th>" + $Names[$x] + "</th>")
    $txtstream.WriteLine("<td         align='left'   nowrap='true'><xsl:value-of
select="" data/" + $Tablename + "/" + $Names[$x] + """/></td></tr>")
}
$txtstream.WriteLine("</table>")
$txtstream.WriteLine("</body>")
$txtstream.WriteLine("</html>")
$txtstream.WriteLine("</xsl:template>")
$txtstream.WriteLine("</xsl:stylesheet>")
$txtstream.Close()

}


$objs = GWMI -namespace root\cimv2 -class Win32_Process
if(! $objs.Count)
{
    $obj = $objs
    $Names=[Array]::CreateInstance([String], $obj.Properties.Count)
    $Value=[Array]::CreateInstance([String], 1, $obj.Properties.Count)

    $x = 0
    $y = 0
```

```
      foreach($prop in $obj.Properties)
      {
        $Names[$x] = $prop.Name
        $Values[0,$x] = GetValue $prop.Name $obj
        $x = $x + 1
      }
   }
   else
   {

      foreach($obj in $objs)
      {
        $Names=[Array]::CreateInstance([String], $obj.Properties.Count)
        $Values=[Array]::CreateInstance([String],                $objs.Count,
$obj.Properties.Count)
        break
      }
      $x = 0
      $y = 0


      foreach($obj in $objs)
      {

        foreach($prop in $obj.Properties)
        {
          $Names[$x] = $prop.Name
          $x = $x + 1
        }
        break
      }
      $x = 0
      foreach($obj in $objs)
      {
        foreach($prop in $obj.Properties)
        {
          $Value = GetValue $prop.Name $obj
          $Values[$y,$x] = $Value
          $x = $x + 1
```

```
      }
      $x=0
      $y = $y + 1
  }

}

WriteTheXSLCode $Names $Values "Process"
```

Multi-Line Vertical

```
$Names
$Values

  function GetValue
  {
    param
    (
    [string]$Name,
    [object]$obj
    )
    [string]$PName = $Name + " = "
    [string]$tempstr = $obj.GetText(0)
    $pos = $tempstr.IndexOf($PName)
    if ($pos -gt 0)
    {
     $pos = $pos + $PName.Length
     $tempstr = $tempstr.SubString($pos, ($tempstr.Length - $pos))
     $pos = $tempstr.IndexOf(";")
     $tempstr = $tempstr.SubString(0, $pos)
     $tempstr = $tempstr.Replace("'", "")
     $tempstr = $tempstr.Replace("}", "")
     $tempstr = $tempstr.Replace("{", "")
     $tempstr = $tempstr.Trim()
     if($tempstr.Length -gt 14)
     {
      if($obj.Properties.Item($Name).Type -eq 101)
      {
        [System.String]$tstr = $tempstr.SubString(4, 2)
```

```
            $tstr = $tstr + "/"
            $tstr = $tstr + $tempstr.SubString(6, 2)
            $tstr = $tstr + "/"
            $tstr = $tstr + $tempstr.SubString(0, 4)
            $tstr = $tstr + " "
            $tstr = $tstr + $tempstr.SubString(8, 2)
            $tstr = $tstr + ":"
            $tstr = $tstr + $tempstr.SubString(10, 2)
            $tstr = $tstr + ":"
            $tstr = $tstr + $tempstr.SubString(12, 2)
            $tempstr = $tstr
          }
        }
        return $tempstr
      }
      else
      {
        return ""
      }
    }

  function WriteTheXSLCode
  {
   param
   (
   [Array]$Names,
   [Array]$Values,
   [String]$Tablename
   )

   $tempstr = ""

   $ws = new-object -com WScript.Shell
   $fso = new-object -com Scripting.FileSystemObject
   $txtstream = $fso.OpenTextFile($ws.CurrentDirectory + "\" + $Tablename +
".xsl", 2, $true, -2)
   $txtstream.WriteLine("<?xml version='1.0' encoding='iso-8859-1'?>")
   $txtstream.WriteLine("<xsl:stylesheet                    version='1.0'
xmlns:xsl='http://www.w3.org/1999/XSL/Transform'>")
   $txtstream.WriteLine("<xsl:template match=""""/"""">")
```

```
$txtstream.WriteLine("<html>")
$txtstream.WriteLine("<head>")
$txtstream.WriteLine("<title>Products</title>")
$txtstream.WriteLine("<style type='text/css'>")
$txtstream.WriteLine("th")
$txtstream.WriteLine("{")
$txtstream.WriteLine("    COLOR: black;")
$txtstream.WriteLine("    BACKGROUND-COLOR: white;")
$txtstream.WriteLine("    FONT-FAMILY:font-family: Cambria, serif;")
$txtstream.WriteLine("    FONT-SIZE: 12px;")
$txtstream.WriteLine("    text-align: left;")
$txtstream.WriteLine("    white-Space: nowrap;")
$txtstream.WriteLine("}")
$txtstream.WriteLine("td")
$txtstream.WriteLine("{")
$txtstream.WriteLine("    COLOR: black;")
$txtstream.WriteLine("    BACKGROUND-COLOR: white;")
$txtstream.WriteLine("    FONT-FAMILY: font-family: Cambria, serif;")
$txtstream.WriteLine("    FONT-SIZE: 12px;")
$txtstream.WriteLine("    text-align: left;")
$txtstream.WriteLine("    white-Space: nowrap;")
$txtstream.WriteLine("}")
$txtstream.WriteLine("div")
$txtstream.WriteLine("{")
$txtstream.WriteLine("    COLOR: black;")
$txtstream.WriteLine("    BACKGROUND-COLOR: white;")
$txtstream.WriteLine("    FONT-FAMILY: font-family: Cambria, serif;")
$txtstream.WriteLine("    FONT-SIZE: 10px;")
$txtstream.WriteLine("    text-align: left;")
$txtstream.WriteLine("    white-Space: nowrap;")
$txtstream.WriteLine("}")
$txtstream.WriteLine("span")
$txtstream.WriteLine("{")
$txtstream.WriteLine("    COLOR: black;")
$txtstream.WriteLine("    BACKGROUND-COLOR: white;")
$txtstream.WriteLine("    FONT-FAMILY: font-family: Cambria, serif;")
$txtstream.WriteLine("    FONT-SIZE: 10px;")
$txtstream.WriteLine("    text-align: left;")
$txtstream.WriteLine("    white-Space: nowrap;")
$txtstream.WriteLine("    display:inline-block;")
```

```
$txtstream.WriteLine("    width: 100%;")
$txtstream.WriteLine("}")
$txtstream.WriteLine("textarea")
$txtstream.WriteLine("{")
$txtstream.WriteLine("    COLOR: black;")
$txtstream.WriteLine("    BACKGROUND-COLOR: white;")
$txtstream.WriteLine("    FONT-FAMILY: font-family: Cambria, serif;")
$txtstream.WriteLine("    FONT-SIZE: 10px;")
$txtstream.WriteLine("    text-align: left;")
$txtstream.WriteLine("    white-Space: nowrap;")
$txtstream.WriteLine("    width: 100%;")
$txtstream.WriteLine("}")
$txtstream.WriteLine("select")
$txtstream.WriteLine("{")
$txtstream.WriteLine("    COLOR: black;")
$txtstream.WriteLine("    BACKGROUND-COLOR: white;")
$txtstream.WriteLine("    FONT-FAMILY: font-family: Cambria, serif;")
$txtstream.WriteLine("    FONT-SIZE: 10px;")
$txtstream.WriteLine("    text-align: left;")
$txtstream.WriteLine("    white-Space: nowrap;")
$txtstream.WriteLine("    width: 100%;")
$txtstream.WriteLine("}")
$txtstream.WriteLine("input")
$txtstream.WriteLine("{")
$txtstream.WriteLine("    COLOR: black;")
$txtstream.WriteLine("    BACKGROUND-COLOR: white;")
$txtstream.WriteLine("    FONT-FAMILY: font-family: Cambria, serif;")
$txtstream.WriteLine("    FONT-SIZE: 12px;")
$txtstream.WriteLine("    text-align: left;")
$txtstream.WriteLine("    display:table-cell;")
$txtstream.WriteLine("    white-Space: nowrap;")
$txtstream.WriteLine("}")
$txtstream.WriteLine("h1 {")
$txtstream.WriteLine("color: antiquewhite;")
$txtstream.WriteLine("text-shadow: 1px 1px 1px black;")
$txtstream.WriteLine("padding: 3px;")
$txtstream.WriteLine("text-align: center;")
$txtstream.WriteLine("box-shadow: invar 2px 2px 5px rgba(0,0,0,0.5), invar -
2px -2px 5px rgba(255,255,255,0.5);")
$txtstream.WriteLine("}")
```

```
$txtstream.WriteLine("</style>")
$txtstream.WriteLine("</head>")
$txtstream.WriteLine("<body>")
$txtstream.WriteLine("<table          border=""0""          Cellpadding=""2""
cellspacing=""2"">")
for($x=0;$x -lt $Names.GetLength(0); $x++)
{
    $txtstream.WriteLine("<tr><th>"   +   $Names[$x]   +   "</th><xsl:for-each
select=""data/" + $Tablename + """"><td  align='left' nowrap='true'><xsl:value-of
select=""" + $Names[$x]  + """"/></td></xsl:for-each></tr>")
}
$txtstream.WriteLine("</table>")
$txtstream.WriteLine("</body>")
$txtstream.WriteLine("</html>")
$txtstream.WriteLine("</xsl:template>")
$txtstream.WriteLine("</xsl:stylesheet>")
$txtstream.Close()

}


$objs = GWMI -namespace root\cimv2 -class Win32_Process
if(! $objs.Count)
{
    $obj = $objs
    $Names=[Array]::CreateInstance([String], $obj.Properties.Count)
    $Value=[Array]::CreateInstance([String], 1, $obj.Properties.Count)

    $x = 0
    $y = 0

    foreach($prop in $obj.Properties)
    {
        $Names[$x] = $prop.Name
        $Values[0,$x] = GetValue $prop.Name $obj
        $x = $x + 1
    }
}
else
{
```

```
foreach($obj in $objs)
{
   $Names=[Array]::CreateInstance([String], $obj.Properties.Count)
   $Values=[Array]::CreateInstance([String], $objs.Count,
$obj.Properties.Count)
   break
}
$x = 0
$y = 0


foreach($obj in $objs)
{

   foreach($prop in $obj.Properties)
   {
      $Names[$x] = $prop.Name
      $x = $x + 1
   }
   break
}
$x = 0
foreach($obj in $objs)
{
   foreach($prop in $obj.Properties)
   {
      $Value = GetValue $prop.Name $obj
      $Values[$y,$x] = $Value
      $x = $x + 1
   }
   $x=0
   $y = $y + 1
}

}

WriteTheXSLCode $Names $Values "Process"
```

When the Element XML for XSL xml file is clicked, it created this:

Caption	CommandLine
System Idle Process	
System	
smss.exe	
csrss.exe	
wininit.exe	wininit.exe
csrss.exe	
services.exe	
lsass.exe	C:\\Windows\\system32\\lsass.exe
svchost.exe	C:\\Windows\\system32\\svchost.exe -k DcomLaunch
winlogon.exe	winlogon.exe
svchost.exe	C:\\Windows\\system32\\svchost.exe -k RPCSS
dwm.exe	\dwm.exe\
NVDisplay.Container.exe	\C:\\Program Files\\NVIDIA Corporation\\Display.NvContainer\\NVDisplay.Container.exe\ -s
svchost.exe	C:\\Windows\\System32\\svchost.exe -k LocalServiceNetworkRestricted
svchost.exe	C:\\Windows\\system32\\svchost.exe -k netsvcs
svchost.exe	C:\\Windows\\system32\\svchost.exe -k LocalService
svchost.exe	C:\\Windows\\system32\\svchost.exe -k NetworkService
svchost.exe	C:\\Windows\\System32\\svchost.exe -k LocalSystemNetworkRestricted
svchost.exe	C:\\Windows\\system32\\svchost.exe -k LocalServiceNoNetwork
spoolsv.exe	C:\\Windows\\System32\\spoolsv.exe
svchost.exe	C:\\Windows\\system32\\svchost.exe -k apphost

Visualizations
CSS rendering of HTML

THE IMAGES BELOW ARE THE RESULT OF THE USE OF THE CSS STYLESHEETS THAT WERE COMBINED WITH THE HTML CODE I WROTE PREVIOUSLY and are examples of the difference between reports and tables.

Report:

Table:

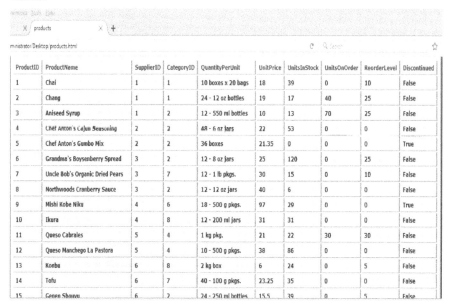

ProductID	ProductName	SupplierID	CategoryID	QuantityPerUnit	UnitPrice	UnitsInStock	UnitsOnOrder	ReorderLevel	Discontinued
1	Chai	1	1	10 boxes x 20 bags	18	39	0	10	False
2	Chang	1	1	24 - 12 oz bottles	19	17	40	25	False
3	Aniseed Syrup	1	2	12 - 550 ml bottles	10	13	70	25	False
4	Chef Anton's Cajun Seasoning	2	2	48 - 6 oz jars	22	53	0	0	False
5	Chef Anton's Gumbo Mix	2	2	36 boxes	21.35	0	0	0	True
6	Grandma's Boysenberry Spread	3	2	12 - 8 oz jars	25	120	0	25	False
7	Uncle Bob's Organic Dried Pears	3	7	12 - 1 lb pkgs.	30	15	0	10	False
8	Northwoods Cranberry Sauce	3	2	12 - 12 oz jars	40	6	0	0	False
9	Mishi Kobe Niku	4	6	18 - 500 g pkgs.	97	29	0	0	True
10	Ikura	4	8	12 - 200 ml jars	31	31	0	0	False
11	Queso Cabrales	5	4	1 kg pkg.	21	22	30	30	False
12	Queso Manchego La Pastora	5	4	10 - 500 g pkgs.	38	86	0	0	False
13	Konbu	6	8	2 kg box	6	24	0	5	False
14	Tofu	6	7	40 - 100 g pkgs.	23.25	35	0	0	False
15	Genen Shouyu	6	2	24 - 250 ml bottles	15.5	39	0	5	False

None:

Black and White

Colored:

AccountExpires	AuthorizationFlags	BadPasswordCount	Caption	CodePage	Comment	CountryCode	Description
			NT AUTHORITY\SYSTEM				Network login profile settings for SYSTEM on NT AUTHORITY
			NT AUTHORITY\LOCAL SERVICE				Network login profile settings for LOCAL SERVICE on NT AUTHORITY
			NT AUTHORITY\NETWORK SERVICE				Network login profile settings for NETWORK SERVICE on NT AUTHORITY
	0	0	Administrator	0	Built-in account for administering the computer/domain	0	Network login profile settings for on WIN-SJRLOAKMF9B
			NT SERVICE\SSASTELEMETRY				Network login profile settings for SSASTELEMETRY on NT SERVICE
			NT SERVICE\SSISTELEMETRY130				Network login profile settings for SSISTELEMETRY130 on NT SERVICE
			NT SERVICE\SQLTELEMETRY				Network login profile settings for SQLTELEMETRY on NT SERVICE
			NT SERVICE\MSSQLServerOLAPService				Network login profile settings for MSSQLServerOLAPService on NT SERVICE
			NT SERVICE\ReportServer				Network login profile settings for ReportServer on NT SERVICE
			NT SERVICE\MSSQLFDLauncher				Network login profile settings for MSSQLFDLauncher on NT SERVICE
			NT SERVICE\MSSQLLaunchpad				Network login profile settings for MSSQLLaunchpad on NT SERVICE
			NT SERVICE\SქlDsServer130				Network login profile settings for SQLDsServer130 on NT SERVICE
			NT SERVICE\MSSQLSERVER				Network login profile settings for MSSQLSERVER on NT SERVICE
			IIS APPPOOL\Classic .NET AppPool				Network login profile settings for Classic .NET AppPool on IIS APPPOOL
			IIS APPPOOL\.NET v4.5				Network login profile settings for .NET v4.5 on IIS APPPOOL
			IIS APPPOOL\.NET v2.0				Network login profile settings for .NET v2.0 on IIS APPPOOL
			IIS APPPOOL\.NET v4.5 Classic				Network login profile settings for .NET v4.5 Classic on IIS APPPOOL
			IIS APPPOOL\.NET v2.0 Classic				Network login profile settings for .NET v2.0 Classic on IIS APPPOOL

Oscillating

Availability	BytesPerSector	Capabilities	CapabilityDescriptions	Caption	CompressionMethod	ConfigManagerErrorCode	ConfigManagerUserConfig
	512	3, 4, 10	Random Access, Supports Writing, SMART Notification	OCZ REVODRIVE350 SCSI Disk Device		0	FALSE
	512	3, 4	Random Access, Supports Writing	NVMe TOSHIBA-RD400		0	FALSE
	512	3, 4, 10	Random Access, Supports Writing, SMART Notification	TOSHIBA DT01ACA200		0	FALSE

3D

Availability	BytesPerSector	Capabilities	CapabilityDescriptions	Caption	CompressionMethod	ConfigManagerErrorCode	ConfigManagerUserConfig	CreationClassName
	512	3, 4, 10	Random Access, Supports Writing, SMART Notification	OCZ REVODRIVE350 SCSI Disk Device		0	FALSE	Win32_DiskDrive
	512	3, 4	Random Access, Supports Writing	NVMe TOSHIBA-RD400		0	FALSE	Win32_DiskDrive
	512	3, 4, 10	Random Access, Supports Writing, SMART Notification	TOSHIBA DT01ACA200		0	FALSE	Win32_DiskDrive

Shadow Box:

Availability	BytesPerSector	Capabilities	CapabilityDescriptions	Caption	CompressionMethod	ConfigManagerErrorCode	ConfigManagerUserConfig	CreationClassName	DefaultBlockSize
	512	3, 4, 10	Random Access, Supports Writing, SMART Notification	OCZ REVODRIVE350 SCSI Disk Device		0	FALSE	Win32_DiskDrive	
	512	3, 4	Random Access, Supports Writing	NVMe TOSHIBA-RD400		0	FALSE	Win32_DiskDrive	
	512	3, 4, 10	Random Access, Supports Writing, SMART Notification	TOSHIBA DT01ACA200		0	FALSE	Win32_DiskDrive	

Shadow Box Single Line Vertical

BiosCharacteristics	7, 10, 11, 12, 15, 16, 17, 19, 23, 24, 25, 26, 27, 28, 29, 32, 33, 40, 42, 43, 48, 50, 58, 59, 64, 65, 66, 67, 68, 69, 70, 71, 72, 73, 74, 75, 76, 77, 78, 79
BIOSVersion	ALASKA - 1072009, 0504, American Megatrends - 5000C
BuildNumber	
Caption	0504
CodeSet	
CurrentLanguage	en|US|iso8859-1
Description	0504
IdentificationCode	
InstallableLanguages	8
InstallDate	
LanguageEdition	
ListOfLanguages	en|US|iso8859-1, fr|FR|iso8859-1, zh|CN|unicode, , , , ,
Manufacturer	American Megatrends Inc.
Name	0504
OtherTargetOS	
PrimaryBIOS	TRUE

Shadow Box Multi line Vertical

Property	Value 1	Value 2	Value 3
Availability			
BytesPerSector	512	512	512
Capabilities	3, 4, 10	3, 4	3, 4, 10
CapabilityDescriptions	Random Access, Supports Writing, SMART Notification	Random Access, Supports Writing	Random Access, Supports Writing, SMART Notification
Caption	OCZ-REVODRIVE350 SCSI Disk Device	NVMe TOSHIBA-RD400	TOSHIBA DT01ACA200
CompressionMethod			
ConfigManagerErrorCode	0	0	0
ConfigManagerUserConfig	FALSE	FALSE	FALSE
CreationClassName	Win32_DiskDrive	Win32_DiskDrive	Win32_DiskDrive
DefaultBlockSize			
Description	Disk drive	Disk drive	Disk drive
DeviceID	\\.\PHYSICALDRIVE2	\\.\PHYSICALDRIVE1	\\.\PHYSICALDRIVE0
ErrorCleared			
ErrorDescription			
ErrorMethodology			
FirmwareRevision	2.50	57CZ4102	MX4OABB0
Index	2	1	0

Appendix A
Stylesheets

don't even pretend to be a stylesheet guru. These are here because I like the way
they look and what they do behind the scenes to get the job done.

NONE

```
txtstream.WriteLine("<style type='text/css'>")
txtstream.WriteLine("th")
txtstream.WriteLine("{")
txtstream.WriteLine("   COLOR: white;")
txtstream.WriteLine("}")
txtstream.WriteLine("td")
txtstream.WriteLine("{")
txtstream.WriteLine("   COLOR: white;")
txtstream.WriteLine("}")
txtstream.WriteLine("</style>")
```

BLACK AND WHITE TEXT

```
$txtstream.WriteLine("<style type='text/css'>")
$txtstream.WriteLine("th")
$txtstream.WriteLine("{")
$txtstream.WriteLine("   COLOR: white;")
$txtstream.WriteLine("   BACKGROUND-COLOR: black;")
```

```
$txtstream.WriteLine("    FONT-FAMILY:font-family: Cambria, serif;")
$txtstream.WriteLine("    FONT-SIZE: 12px;")
$txtstream.WriteLine("    text-align: left;")
$txtstream.WriteLine("    white-Space: nowrap;")
$txtstream.WriteLine("}")
$txtstream.WriteLine("td")
$txtstream.WriteLine("{")
$txtstream.WriteLine("    COLOR: white;")
$txtstream.WriteLine("    BACKGROUND-COLOR: black;")
$txtstream.WriteLine("    FONT-FAMILY: font-family: Cambria, serif;")
$txtstream.WriteLine("    FONT-SIZE: 12px;")
$txtstream.WriteLine("    text-align: left;")
$txtstream.WriteLine("    white-Space: nowrap;")
$txtstream.WriteLine("}")
$txtstream.WriteLine("div")
$txtstream.WriteLine("{")
$txtstream.WriteLine("    COLOR: white;")
$txtstream.WriteLine("    BACKGROUND-COLOR: black;")
$txtstream.WriteLine("    FONT-FAMILY: font-family: Cambria, serif;")
$txtstream.WriteLine("    FONT-SIZE: 10px;")
$txtstream.WriteLine("    text-align: left;")
$txtstream.WriteLine("    white-Space: nowrap;")
$txtstream.WriteLine("}")
$txtstream.WriteLine("span")
$txtstream.WriteLine("{")
$txtstream.WriteLine("    COLOR: white;")
$txtstream.WriteLine("    BACKGROUND-COLOR: black;")
$txtstream.WriteLine("    FONT-FAMILY: font-family: Cambria, serif;")
$txtstream.WriteLine("    FONT-SIZE: 10px;")
$txtstream.WriteLine("    text-align: left;")
$txtstream.WriteLine("    white-Space: nowrap;")
$txtstream.WriteLine("    display:inline-block;")
$txtstream.WriteLine("    width: 100%;")
$txtstream.WriteLine("}")
$txtstream.WriteLine("textarea")
$txtstream.WriteLine("{")
$txtstream.WriteLine("    COLOR: white;")
$txtstream.WriteLine("    BACKGROUND-COLOR: black;")
$txtstream.WriteLine("    FONT-FAMILY: font-family: Cambria, serif;")
$txtstream.WriteLine("    FONT-SIZE: 10px;")
```

```
$txtstream.WriteLine("    text-align: left;")
$txtstream.WriteLine("    white-Space: nowrap;")
$txtstream.WriteLine("    width: 100%;")
$txtstream.WriteLine("}")
$txtstream.WriteLine("select")
$txtstream.WriteLine("{")
$txtstream.WriteLine("    COLOR: white;")
$txtstream.WriteLine("    BACKGROUND-COLOR: black;")
$Lxtstream.WritcLine("    FONT-FAMILY: font-family: Cambria, serif;")
$txtstream.WriteLine("    FONT-SIZE: 10px;")
$txtstream.WriteLine("    text-align: left;")
$txtstream.WriteLine("    white-Space: nowrap;")
$txtstream.WriteLine("    width: 100%;")
$txtstream.WriteLine("}")
$txtstream.WriteLine("input")
$txtstream.WriteLine("{")
$txtstream.WriteLine("    COLOR: white;")
$txtstream.WriteLine("    BACKGROUND-COLOR: black;")
$txtstream.WriteLine("    FONT-FAMILY: font-family: Cambria, serif;")
$txtstream.WriteLine("    FONT-SIZE: 12px;")
$txtstream.WriteLine("    text-align: left;")
$txtstream.WriteLine("    display:table-cell;")
$txtstream.WriteLine("    white-Space: nowrap;")
$txtstream.WriteLine("}")
$txtstream.WriteLine("h1 {")
$txtstream.WriteLine("color: antiquewhite;")
$txtstream.WriteLine("text-shadow: 1px 1px 1px black;")
$txtstream.WriteLine("padding: 3px;")
$txtstream.WriteLine("text-align: center;")
$txtstream.WriteLine("box-shadow: invar 2px 2px 5px rgba(0,0,0,0.5), invar -
2px -2px 5px rgba(255,255,255,0.5);")
$txtstream.WriteLine("}")
$txtstream.WriteLine("</style>")
```

COLORED TEXT

```
$txtstream.WriteLine("<style type='text/css'>")
$txtstream.WriteLine("th")
$txtstream.WriteLine("{")
$txtstream.WriteLine("    COLOR: darkred;")
```

```
$txtstream.WriteLine("    BACKGROUND-COLOR: #eeeeee;")
$txtstream.WriteLine("    FONT-FAMILY:font-family: Cambria, serif;")
$txtstream.WriteLine("    FONT-SIZE: 12px;")
$txtstream.WriteLine("    text-align: left;")
$txtstream.WriteLine("    white-Space: nowrap;")
$txtstream.WriteLine("}")
$txtstream.WriteLine("td")
$txtstream.WriteLine("{")
$txtstream.WriteLine("    COLOR: navy;")
$txtstream.WriteLine("    BACKGROUND-COLOR: #eeeeee;")
$txtstream.WriteLine("    FONT-FAMILY: font-family: Cambria, serif;")
$txtstream.WriteLine("    FONT-SIZE: 12px;")
$txtstream.WriteLine("    text-align: left;")
$txtstream.WriteLine("    white-Space: nowrap;")
$txtstream.WriteLine("}")
$txtstream.WriteLine("div")
$txtstream.WriteLine("{")
$txtstream.WriteLine("    COLOR: white;")
$txtstream.WriteLine("    BACKGROUND-COLOR: navy;")
$txtstream.WriteLine("    FONT-FAMILY: font-family: Cambria, serif;")
$txtstream.WriteLine("    FONT-SIZE: 10px;")
$txtstream.WriteLine("    text-align: left;")
$txtstream.WriteLine("    white-Space: nowrap;")
$txtstream.WriteLine("}")
$txtstream.WriteLine("span")
$txtstream.WriteLine("{")
$txtstream.WriteLine("    COLOR: white;")
$txtstream.WriteLine("    BACKGROUND-COLOR: navy;")
$txtstream.WriteLine("    FONT-FAMILY: font-family: Cambria, serif;")
$txtstream.WriteLine("    FONT-SIZE: 10px;")
$txtstream.WriteLine("    text-align: left;")
$txtstream.WriteLine("    white-Space: nowrap;")
$txtstream.WriteLine("    display:inline-block;")
$txtstream.WriteLine("    width: 100%;")
$txtstream.WriteLine("}")
$txtstream.WriteLine("textarea")
$txtstream.WriteLine("{")
$txtstream.WriteLine("    COLOR: white;")
$txtstream.WriteLine("    BACKGROUND-COLOR: navy;")
$txtstream.WriteLine("    FONT-FAMILY: font-family: Cambria, serif;")
```

```
$txtstream.WriteLine("    FONT-SIZE: 10px;")
$txtstream.WriteLine("    text-align: left;")
$txtstream.WriteLine("    white-Space: nowrap;")
$txtstream.WriteLine("    width: 100%;")
$txtstream.WriteLine("}")
$txtstream.WriteLine("select")
$txtstream.WriteLine("{")
$txtstream.WriteLine("    COLOR: white;")
$txtstream.WriteLine("    BACKGROUND-COLOR: navy;")
$txtstream.WriteLine("    FONT-FAMILY: font-family: Cambria, serif;")
$txtstream.WriteLine("    FONT-SIZE: 10px;")
$txtstream.WriteLine("    text-align: left;")
$txtstream.WriteLine("    white-Space: nowrap;")
$txtstream.WriteLine("    width: 100%;")
$txtstream.WriteLine("}")
$txtstream.WriteLine("input")
$txtstream.WriteLine("{")
$txtstream.WriteLine("    COLOR: white;")
$txtstream.WriteLine("    BACKGROUND-COLOR: navy;")
$txtstream.WriteLine("    FONT-FAMILY: font-family: Cambria, serif;")
$txtstream.WriteLine("    FONT-SIZE: 12px;")
$txtstream.WriteLine("    text-align: left;")
$txtstream.WriteLine("    display:table-cell;")
$txtstream.WriteLine("    white-Space: nowrap;")
$txtstream.WriteLine("}")
$txtstream.WriteLine("h1 {")
$txtstream.WriteLine("color: antiquewhite;")
$txtstream.WriteLine("text-shadow: 1px 1px 1px black;")
$txtstream.WriteLine("padding: 3px;")
$txtstream.WriteLine("text-align: center;")
$txtstream.WriteLine("box-shadow: invar 2px 2px 5px rgba(0,0,0,0.5), invar -
2px -2px 5px rgba(255,255,255,0.5);")
$txtstream.WriteLine("}")
$txtstream.WriteLine("</style>")
```

OSCILLATING ROW COLORS

```
$txtstream.WriteLine("<style>")
```

```
$txtstream.WriteLine("th")
$txtstream.WriteLine("{")
$txtstream.WriteLine("    COLOR: white;")
$txtstream.WriteLine("    BACKGROUND-COLOR: navy;")
$txtstream.WriteLine("    FONT-FAMILY:font-family: Cambria, serif;")
$txtstream.WriteLine("    FONT-SIZE: 12px;")
$txtstream.WriteLine("    text-align: left;")
$txtstream.WriteLine("    white-Space: nowrap;")
$txtstream.WriteLine("}")
$txtstream.WriteLine("td")
$txtstream.WriteLine("{")
$txtstream.WriteLine("    COLOR: navy;")
$txtstream.WriteLine("    FONT-FAMILY: font-family: Cambria, serif;")
$txtstream.WriteLine("    FONT-SIZE: 12px;")
$txtstream.WriteLine("    text-align: left;")
$txtstream.WriteLine("    white-Space: nowrap;")
$txtstream.WriteLine("}")
$txtstream.WriteLine("div")
$txtstream.WriteLine("{")
$txtstream.WriteLine("    COLOR: navy;")
$txtstream.WriteLine("    FONT-FAMILY: font-family: Cambria, serif;")
$txtstream.WriteLine("    FONT-SIZE: 12px;")
$txtstream.WriteLine("    text-align: left;")
$txtstream.WriteLine("    white-Space: nowrap;")
$txtstream.WriteLine("}")
$txtstream.WriteLine("span")
$txtstream.WriteLine("{")
$txtstream.WriteLine("    COLOR: navy;")
$txtstream.WriteLine("    FONT-FAMILY: font-family: Cambria, serif;")
$txtstream.WriteLine("    FONT-SIZE: 12px;")
$txtstream.WriteLine("    text-align: left;")
$txtstream.WriteLine("    white-Space: nowrap;")
$txtstream.WriteLine("    width: 100%;")
$txtstream.WriteLine("}")
$txtstream.WriteLine("textarea")
$txtstream.WriteLine("{")
$txtstream.WriteLine("    COLOR: navy;")
$txtstream.WriteLine("    FONT-FAMILY: font-family: Cambria, serif;")
$txtstream.WriteLine("    FONT-SIZE: 12px;")
$txtstream.WriteLine("    text-align: left;")
```

```
$txtstream.WriteLine("   white-Space: nowrap;")
$txtstream.WriteLine("   display:inline-block;")
$txtstream.WriteLine("   width: 100%;")
$txtstream.WriteLine("}")
$txtstream.WriteLine("select")
$txtstream.WriteLine("{")
$txtstream.WriteLine("   COLOR: navy;")
$txtstream.WriteLine("   FONT-FAMILY: font-family: Cambria, serif;")
$txtstream.WriteLine("   FONT-SIZE: 10px;")
$txtstream.WriteLine("   text-align: left;")
$txtstream.WriteLine("   white-Space: nowrap;")
$txtstream.WriteLine("   display:inline-block;")
$txtstream.WriteLine("   width: 100%;")
$txtstream.WriteLine("}")
$txtstream.WriteLine("input")
$txtstream.WriteLine("{")
$txtstream.WriteLine("   COLOR: navy;")
$txtstream.WriteLine("   FONT-FAMILY: font-family: Cambria, serif;")
$txtstream.WriteLine("   FONT-SIZE: 12px;")
$txtstream.WriteLine("   text-align: left;")
$txtstream.WriteLine("   display:table-cell;")
$txtstream.WriteLine("   white-Space: nowrap;")
$txtstream.WriteLine("}")
$txtstream.WriteLine("h1 {")
$txtstream.WriteLine("color: antiquewhite;")
$txtstream.WriteLine("text-shadow: 1px 1px 1px black;")
$txtstream.WriteLine("padding: 3px;")
$txtstream.WriteLine("text-align: center;")
$txtstream.WriteLine("box-shadow: invar 2px 2px 5px rgba(0,0,0,0.5), invar -
2px -2px 5px rgba(255,255,255,0.5);")
$txtstream.WriteLine("}")
$txtstream.WriteLine("tr:nth-child(even){background-color:#f2f2f2;}")
$txtstream.WriteLine("tr:nth-child(odd){background-color:#cccccc;
color:#f2f2f2;}")
$txtstream.WriteLine("</style>")
```

GHOST DECORATED

```
$txtstream.WriteLine("<style type='text/css'>")
$txtstream.WriteLine("th")
```

```
$txtstream.WriteLine("{")
$txtstream.WriteLine("   COLOR: black;")
$txtstream.WriteLine("   BACKGROUND-COLOR: white;")
$txtstream.WriteLine("   FONT-FAMILY:font-family: Cambria, serif;")
$txtstream.WriteLine("   FONT-SIZE: 12px;")
$txtstream.WriteLine("   text-align: left;")
$txtstream.WriteLine("   white-Space: nowrap;")
$txtstream.WriteLine("}")
$txtstream.WriteLine("td")
$txtstream.WriteLine("{")
$txtstream.WriteLine("   COLOR: black;")
$txtstream.WriteLine("   BACKGROUND-COLOR: white;")
$txtstream.WriteLine("   FONT-FAMILY: font-family: Cambria, serif;")
$txtstream.WriteLine("   FONT-SIZE: 12px;")
$txtstream.WriteLine("   text-align: left;")
$txtstream.WriteLine("   white-Space: nowrap;")
$txtstream.WriteLine("}")
$txtstream.WriteLine("div")
$txtstream.WriteLine("{")
$txtstream.WriteLine("   COLOR: black;")
$txtstream.WriteLine("   BACKGROUND-COLOR: white;")
$txtstream.WriteLine("   FONT-FAMILY: font-family: Cambria, serif;")
$txtstream.WriteLine("   FONT-SIZE: 10px;")
$txtstream.WriteLine("   text-align: left;")
$txtstream.WriteLine("   white-Space: nowrap;")
$txtstream.WriteLine("}")
$txtstream.WriteLine("span")
$txtstream.WriteLine("{")
$txtstream.WriteLine("   COLOR: black;")
$txtstream.WriteLine("   BACKGROUND-COLOR: white;")
$txtstream.WriteLine("   FONT-FAMILY: font-family: Cambria, serif;")
$txtstream.WriteLine("   FONT-SIZE: 10px;")
$txtstream.WriteLine("   text-align: left;")
$txtstream.WriteLine("   white-Space: nowrap;")
$txtstream.WriteLine("   display:inline-block;")
$txtstream.WriteLine("   width: 100%;")
$txtstream.WriteLine("}")
$txtstream.WriteLine("textarea")
$txtstream.WriteLine("{")
$txtstream.WriteLine("   COLOR: black;")
```

```
$txtstream.WriteLine("   BACKGROUND-COLOR: white;")
$txtstream.WriteLine("   FONT-FAMILY: font-family: Cambria, serif;")
$txtstream.WriteLine("   FONT-SIZE: 10px;")
$txtstream.WriteLine("   text-align: left;")
$txtstream.WriteLine("   white-Space: nowrap;")
$txtstream.WriteLine("   width: 100%;")
$txtstream.WriteLine("}")
$txtstream.WriteLine("select")
$txtstrcam.WriteLine("{")
$txtstream.WriteLine("   COLOR: black;")
$txtstream.WriteLine("   BACKGROUND-COLOR: white;")
$txtstream.WriteLine("   FONT-FAMILY: font-family: Cambria, serif;")
$txtstream.WriteLine("   FONT-SIZE: 10px;")
$txtstream.WriteLine("   text-align: left;")
$txtstream.WriteLine("   white-Space: nowrap;")
$txtstream.WriteLine("   width: 100%;")
$txtstream.WriteLine("}")
$txtstream.WriteLine("input")
$txtstream.WriteLine("{")
$txtstream.WriteLine("   COLOR: black;")
$txtstream.WriteLine("   BACKGROUND-COLOR: white;")
$txtstream.WriteLine("   FONT-FAMILY: font-family: Cambria, serif;")
$txtstream.WriteLine("   FONT-SIZE: 12px;")
$txtstream.WriteLine("   text-align: left;")
$txtstream.WriteLine("   display:table-cell;")
$txtstream.WriteLine("   white-Space: nowrap;")
$txtstream.WriteLine("}")
$txtstream.WriteLine("h1 {")
$txtstream.WriteLine("color: antiquewhite;")
$txtstream.WriteLine("text-shadow: 1px 1px 1px black;")
$txtstream.WriteLine("padding: 3px;")
$txtstream.WriteLine("text-align: center;")
$txtstream.WriteLine("box-shadow: invar 2px 2px 5px rgba(0,0,0,0.5), invar -2px -2px 5px rgba(255,255,255,0.5);")
$txtstream.WriteLine("}")
$txtstream.WriteLine("</style>")
```

3D

```
$txtstream.WriteLine("<style type='text/css'>")
$txtstream.WriteLine("body")
$txtstream.WriteLine("{")
$txtstream.WriteLine("   PADDING-RIGHT: 0px;")
$txtstream.WriteLine("   PADDING-LEFT: 0px;")
$txtstream.WriteLine("   PADDING-BOTTOM: 0px;")
$txtstream.WriteLine("   MARGIN: 0px;")
$txtstream.WriteLine("   COLOR: #333;")
$txtstream.WriteLine("   PADDING-TOP: 0px;")
$txtstream.WriteLine("   FONT-FAMILY: verdana, arial, helvetica, sans-serif;")
$txtstream.WriteLine("}")
$txtstream.WriteLine("table")
$txtstream.WriteLine("{")
$txtstream.WriteLine("   BORDER-RIGHT: #999999 3px solid;")
$txtstream.WriteLine("   PADDING-RIGHT: 6px;")
$txtstream.WriteLine("   PADDING-LEFT: 6px;")
$txtstream.WriteLine("   FONT-WEIGHT: Bold;")
$txtstream.WriteLine("   FONT-SIZE: 14px;")
$txtstream.WriteLine("   PADDING-BOTTOM: 6px;")
$txtstream.WriteLine("   COLOR: Peru;")
$txtstream.WriteLine("   LINE-HEIGHT: 14px;")
$txtstream.WriteLine("   PADDING-TOP: 6px;")
$txtstream.WriteLine("   BORDER-BOTTOM: #999 1px solid;")
$txtstream.WriteLine("   BACKGROUND-COLOR: #eeeeee;")
$txtstream.WriteLine("   FONT-FAMILY: verdana, arial, helvetica, sans-serif;")
$txtstream.WriteLine("   FONT-SIZE: 12px;")
$txtstream.WriteLine("}")
$txtstream.WriteLine("th")
$txtstream.WriteLine("{")
$txtstream.WriteLine("   BORDER-RIGHT: #999999 3px solid;")
$txtstream.WriteLine("   PADDING-RIGHT: 6px;")
$txtstream.WriteLine("   PADDING-LEFT: 6px;")
$txtstream.WriteLine("   FONT-WEIGHT: Bold;")
$txtstream.WriteLine("   FONT-SIZE: 14px;")
$txtstream.WriteLine("   PADDING-BOTTOM: 6px;")
$txtstream.WriteLine("   COLOR: darkred;")
$txtstream.WriteLine("   LINE-HEIGHT: 14px;")
$txtstream.WriteLine("   PADDING-TOP: 6px;")
$txtstream.WriteLine("   BORDER-BOTTOM: #999 1px solid;")
$txtstream.WriteLine("   BACKGROUND-COLOR: #eeeeee;")
```

```
$txtstream.WriteLine("    FONT-FAMILY:font-family: Cambria, serif;")
$txtstream.WriteLine("    FONT-SIZE: 12px;")
$txtstream.WriteLine("    text-align: left;")
$txtstream.WriteLine("    white-Space: nowrap;")
$txtstream.WriteLine("}")
$txtstream.WriteLine(".th")
$txtstream.WriteLine("{")
$txtstream.WriteLine("    BORDER-RIGHT: #999999 2px solid;")
$txtstream.WriteLine("    PADDING-RIGHT: 6px;")
$txtstream.WriteLine("    PADDING-LEFT: 6px;")
$txtstream.WriteLine("    FONT-WEIGHT: Bold;")
$txtstream.WriteLine("    PADDING-BOTTOM: 6px;")
$txtstream.WriteLine("    COLOR: black;")
$txtstream.WriteLine("    PADDING-TOP: 6px;")
$txtstream.WriteLine("    BORDER-BOTTOM: #999 2px solid;")
$txtstream.WriteLine("    BACKGROUND-COLOR: #eeeeee;")
$txtstream.WriteLine("    FONT-FAMILY: font-family: Cambria, serif;")
$txtstream.WriteLine("    FONT-SIZE: 10px;")
$txtstream.WriteLine("    text-align: right;")
$txtstream.WriteLine("    white-Space: nowrap;")
$txtstream.WriteLine("}")
$txtstream.WriteLine("td")
$txtstream.WriteLine("{")
$txtstream.WriteLine("    BORDER-RIGHT: #999999 3px solid;")
$txtstream.WriteLine("    PADDING-RIGHT: 6px;")
$txtstream.WriteLine("    PADDING-LEFT: 6px;")
$txtstream.WriteLine("    FONT-WEIGHT: Normal;")
$txtstream.WriteLine("    PADDING-BOTTOM: 6px;")
$txtstream.WriteLine("    COLOR: navy;")
$txtstream.WriteLine("    LINE-HEIGHT: 14px;")
$txtstream.WriteLine("    PADDING-TOP: 6px;")
$txtstream.WriteLine("    BORDER-BOTTOM: #999 1px solid;")
$txtstream.WriteLine("    BACKGROUND-COLOR: #eeeeee;")
$txtstream.WriteLine("    FONT-FAMILY: font-family: Cambria, serif;")
$txtstream.WriteLine("    FONT-SIZE: 12px;")
$txtstream.WriteLine("    text-align: left;")
$txtstream.WriteLine("    white-Space: nowrap;")
$txtstream.WriteLine("}")
$txtstream.WriteLine("div")
$txtstream.WriteLine("{")
```

```
$txtstream.WriteLine("    BORDER-RIGHT: #999999 3px solid;")
$txtstream.WriteLine("    PADDING-RIGHT: 6px;")
$txtstream.WriteLine("    PADDING-LEFT: 6px;")
$txtstream.WriteLine("    FONT-WEIGHT: Normal;")
$txtstream.WriteLine("    PADDING-BOTTOM: 6px;")
$txtstream.WriteLine("    COLOR: white;")
$txtstream.WriteLine("    PADDING-TOP: 6px;")
$txtstream.WriteLine("    BORDER-BOTTOM: #999 1px solid;")
$txtstream.WriteLine("    BACKGROUND-COLOR: navy;")
$txtstream.WriteLine("    FONT-FAMILY: font-family: Cambria, serif;")
$txtstream.WriteLine("    FONT-SIZE: 10px;")
$txtstream.WriteLine("    text-align: left;")
$txtstream.WriteLine("    white-Space: nowrap;")
$txtstream.WriteLine("}")
$txtstream.WriteLine("span")
$txtstream.WriteLine("{")
$txtstream.WriteLine("    BORDER-RIGHT: #999999 3px solid;")
$txtstream.WriteLine("    PADDING-RIGHT: 3px;")
$txtstream.WriteLine("    PADDING-LEFT: 3px;")
$txtstream.WriteLine("    FONT-WEIGHT: Normal;")
$txtstream.WriteLine("    PADDING-BOTTOM: 3px;")
$txtstream.WriteLine("    COLOR: white;")
$txtstream.WriteLine("    PADDING-TOP: 3px;")
$txtstream.WriteLine("    BORDER-BOTTOM: #999 1px solid;")
$txtstream.WriteLine("    BACKGROUND-COLOR: navy;")
$txtstream.WriteLine("    FONT-FAMILY: font-family: Cambria, serif;")
$txtstream.WriteLine("    FONT-SIZE: 10px;")
$txtstream.WriteLine("    text-align: left;")
$txtstream.WriteLine("    white-Space: nowrap;")
$txtstream.WriteLine("    display:inline-block;")
$txtstream.WriteLine("    width: 100%;")
$txtstream.WriteLine("}")
$txtstream.WriteLine("textarea")
$txtstream.WriteLine("{")
$txtstream.WriteLine("    BORDER-RIGHT: #999999 3px solid;")
$txtstream.WriteLine("    PADDING-RIGHT: 3px;")
$txtstream.WriteLine("    PADDING-LEFT: 3px;")
$txtstream.WriteLine("    FONT-WEIGHT: Normal;")
$txtstream.WriteLine("    PADDING-BOTTOM: 3px;")
$txtstream.WriteLine("    COLOR: white;")
```

```
$txtstream.WriteLine("    PADDING-TOP: 3px;")
$txtstream.WriteLine("    BORDER-BOTTOM: #999 1px solid;")
$txtstream.WriteLine("    BACKGROUND-COLOR: navy;")
$txtstream.WriteLine("    FONT-FAMILY: font-family: Cambria, serif;")
$txtstream.WriteLine("    FONT-SIZE: 10px;")
$txtstream.WriteLine("    text-align: left;")
$txtstream.WriteLine("    white-Space: nowrap;")
$txtstream.WriteLine("    width: 100%;")
$txtstream.WriteLine("}")
$txtstream.WriteLine("select")
$txtstream.WriteLine("{")
$txtstream.WriteLine("    BORDER-RIGHT: #999999 3px solid;")
$txtstream.WriteLine("    PADDING-RIGHT: 6px;")
$txtstream.WriteLine("    PADDING-LEFT: 6px;")
$txtstream.WriteLine("    FONT-WEIGHT: Normal;")
$txtstream.WriteLine("    PADDING-BOTTOM: 6px;")
$txtstream.WriteLine("    COLOR: white;")
$txtstream.WriteLine("    PADDING-TOP: 6px;")
$txtstream.WriteLine("    BORDER-BOTTOM: #999 1px solid;")
$txtstream.WriteLine("    BACKGROUND-COLOR: navy;")
$txtstream.WriteLine("    FONT-FAMILY: font-family: Cambria, serif;")
$txtstream.WriteLine("    FONT-SIZE: 10px;")
$txtstream.WriteLine("    text-align: left;")
$txtstream.WriteLine("    white-Space: nowrap;")
$txtstream.WriteLine("    width: 100%;")
$txtstream.WriteLine("}")
$txtstream.WriteLine("input")
$txtstream.WriteLine("{")
$txtstream.WriteLine("    BORDER-RIGHT: #999999 3px solid;")
$txtstream.WriteLine("    PADDING-RIGHT: 3px;")
$txtstream.WriteLine("    PADDING-LEFT: 3px;")
$txtstream.WriteLine("    FONT-WEIGHT: Bold;")
$txtstream.WriteLine("    PADDING-BOTTOM: 3px;")
$txtstream.WriteLine("    COLOR: white;")
$txtstream.WriteLine("    PADDING-TOP: 3px;")
$txtstream.WriteLine("    BORDER-BOTTOM: #999 1px solid;")
$txtstream.WriteLine("    BACKGROUND-COLOR: navy;")
$txtstream.WriteLine("    FONT-FAMILY: font-family: Cambria, serif;")
$txtstream.WriteLine("    FONT-SIZE: 12px;")
$txtstream.WriteLine("    text-align: left;")
```

```
$txtstream.WriteLine("    display:table-cell;")
$txtstream.WriteLine("    white-Space: nowrap;")
$txtstream.WriteLine("    width: 100%;")
$txtstream.WriteLine("}")
$txtstream.WriteLine("h1 {")
$txtstream.WriteLine("color: antiquewhite;")
$txtstream.WriteLine("text-shadow: 1px 1px 1px black;")
$txtstream.WriteLine("padding: 3px;")
$txtstream.WriteLine("text-align: center;")
$txtstream.WriteLine("box-shadow: invar 2px 2px 5px rgba(0,0,0,0.5), invar -
2px -2px 5px rgba(255,255,255,0.5);")
$txtstream.WriteLine("}")
$txtstream.WriteLine("</style>")
```

SHADOW BOX

```
$txtstream.WriteLine("<style type='text/css'>")
$txtstream.WriteLine("body")
$txtstream.WriteLine("{")
$txtstream.WriteLine("    PADDING-RIGHT: 0px;")
$txtstream.WriteLine("    PADDING-LEFT: 0px;")
$txtstream.WriteLine("    PADDING-BOTTOM: 0px;")
$txtstream.WriteLine("    MARGIN: 0px;")
$txtstream.WriteLine("    COLOR: #333;")
$txtstream.WriteLine("    PADDING-TOP: 0px;")
$txtstream.WriteLine("    FONT-FAMILY: verdana, arial, helvetica, sans-serif;")
$txtstream.WriteLine("}")
$txtstream.WriteLine("table")
$txtstream.WriteLine("{")
$txtstream.WriteLine("    BORDER-RIGHT: #999999 1px solid;")
$txtstream.WriteLine("    PADDING-RIGHT: 1px;")
$txtstream.WriteLine("    PADDING-LEFT: 1px;")
$txtstream.WriteLine("    PADDING-BOTTOM: 1px;")
$txtstream.WriteLine("    LINE-HEIGHT: 8px;")
$txtstream.WriteLine("    PADDING-TOP: 1px;")
$txtstream.WriteLine("    BORDER-BOTTOM: #999 1px solid;")
$txtstream.WriteLine("    BACKGROUND-COLOR: #eeeeee;")
$txtstream.WriteLine("
filter:progid:DXImageTransform.Microsoft.Shadow(color='silver',    Direction=135,
Strength=16)")
```

```
$txtstream.WriteLine("}")
$txtstream.WriteLine("th")
$txtstream.WriteLine("{")
$txtstream.WriteLine("    BORDER-RIGHT: #999999 3px solid;")
$txtstream.WriteLine("    PADDING-RIGHT: 6px;")
$txtstream.WriteLine("    PADDING-LEFT: 6px;")
$txtstream.WriteLine("    FONT-WEIGHT: Bold;")
$txtstream.WriteLine("    FONT-SIZE: 14px;")
$txtstream.WriteLine("    PADDING-BOTTOM: 6px;")
$txtstream.WriteLine("    COLOR: darkred;")
$txtstream.WriteLine("    LINE-HEIGHT: 14px;")
$txtstream.WriteLine("    PADDING-TOP: 6px;")
$txtstream.WriteLine("    BORDER-BOTTOM: #999 1px solid;")
$txtstream.WriteLine("    BACKGROUND-COLOR: #eeeeee;")
$txtstream.WriteLine("    FONT-FAMILY: font-family: Cambria, serif;")
$txtstream.WriteLine("    FONT-SIZE: 12px;")
$txtstream.WriteLine("    text-align: left;")
$txtstream.WriteLine("    white-Space: nowrap;")
$txtstream.WriteLine("}")
$txtstream.WriteLine(".th")
$txtstream.WriteLine("{")
$txtstream.WriteLine("    BORDER-RIGHT: #999999 2px solid;")
$txtstream.WriteLine("    PADDING-RIGHT: 6px;")
$txtstream.WriteLine("    PADDING-LEFT: 6px;")
$txtstream.WriteLine("    FONT-WEIGHT: Bold;")
$txtstream.WriteLine("    PADDING-BOTTOM: 6px;")
$txtstream.WriteLine("    COLOR: black;")
$txtstream.WriteLine("    PADDING-TOP: 6px;")
$txtstream.WriteLine("    BORDER-BOTTOM: #999 2px solid;")
$txtstream.WriteLine("    BACKGROUND-COLOR: #eeeeee;")
$txtstream.WriteLine("    FONT-FAMILY: font-family: Cambria, serif;")
$txtstream.WriteLine("    FONT-SIZE: 10px;")
$txtstream.WriteLine("    text-align: right;")
$txtstream.WriteLine("    white-Space: nowrap;")
$txtstream.WriteLine("}")
$txtstream.WriteLine("td")
$txtstream.WriteLine("{")
$txtstream.WriteLine("    BORDER-RIGHT: #999999 3px solid;")
$txtstream.WriteLine("    PADDING-RIGHT: 6px;")
$txtstream.WriteLine("    PADDING-LEFT: 6px;")
```

```
$txtstream.WriteLine("    FONT-WEIGHT: Normal;")
$txtstream.WriteLine("    PADDING-BOTTOM: 6px;")
$txtstream.WriteLine("    COLOR: navy;")
$txtstream.WriteLine("    LINE-HEIGHT: 14px;")
$txtstream.WriteLine("    PADDING-TOP: 6px;")
$txtstream.WriteLine("    BORDER-BOTTOM: #999 1px solid;")
$txtstream.WriteLine("    BACKGROUND-COLOR: #eeeeee;")
$txtstream.WriteLine("    FONT-FAMILY: font-family: Cambria, serif;")
$txtstream.WriteLine("    FONT-SIZE: 12px;")
$txtstream.WriteLine("    text-align: left;")
$txtstream.WriteLine("    white-Space: nowrap;")
$txtstream.WriteLine("}")
$txtstream.WriteLine("div")
$txtstream.WriteLine("{")
$txtstream.WriteLine("    BORDER-RIGHT: #999999 3px solid;")
$txtstream.WriteLine("    PADDING-RIGHT: 6px;")
$txtstream.WriteLine("    PADDING-LEFT: 6px;")
$txtstream.WriteLine("    FONT-WEIGHT: Normal;")
$txtstream.WriteLine("    PADDING-BOTTOM: 6px;")
$txtstream.WriteLine("    COLOR: white;")
$txtstream.WriteLine("    PADDING-TOP: 6px;")
$txtstream.WriteLine("    BORDER-BOTTOM: #999 1px solid;")
$txtstream.WriteLine("    BACKGROUND-COLOR: navy;")
$txtstream.WriteLine("    FONT-FAMILY: font-family: Cambria, serif;")
$txtstream.WriteLine("    FONT-SIZE: 10px;")
$txtstream.WriteLine("    text-align: left;")
$txtstream.WriteLine("    white-Space: nowrap;")
$txtstream.WriteLine("}")
$txtstream.WriteLine("span")
$txtstream.WriteLine("{")
$txtstream.WriteLine("    BORDER-RIGHT: #999999 3px solid;")
$txtstream.WriteLine("    PADDING-RIGHT: 3px;")
$txtstream.WriteLine("    PADDING-LEFT: 3px;")
$txtstream.WriteLine("    FONT-WEIGHT: Normal;")
$txtstream.WriteLine("    PADDING-BOTTOM: 3px;")
$txtstream.WriteLine("    COLOR: white;")
$txtstream.WriteLine("    PADDING-TOP: 3px;")
$txtstream.WriteLine("    BORDER-BOTTOM: #999 1px solid;")
$txtstream.WriteLine("    BACKGROUND-COLOR: navy;")
$txtstream.WriteLine("    FONT-FAMILY: font-family: Cambria, serif;")
```

```
$txtstream.WriteLine("   FONT-SIZE: 10px;")
$txtstream.WriteLine("   text-align: left;")
$txtstream.WriteLine("   white-Space: nowrap;")
$txtstream.WriteLine("   display: inline-block;")
$txtstream.WriteLine("   width: 100%;")
$txtstream.WriteLine("}")
$txtstream.WriteLine("textarea")
$txtstream.WriteLine("{")
$txtstream.WriteLine("   BORDER-RIGHT: #999999 3px solid;")
$txtstream.WriteLine("   PADDING-RIGHT: 3px;")
$txtstream.WriteLine("   PADDING-LEFT: 3px;")
$txtstream.WriteLine("   FONT-WEIGHT: Normal;")
$txtstream.WriteLine("   PADDING-BOTTOM: 3px;")
$txtstream.WriteLine("   COLOR: white;")
$txtstream.WriteLine("   PADDING-TOP: 3px;")
$txtstream.WriteLine("   BORDER-BOTTOM: #999 1px solid;")
$txtstream.WriteLine("   BACKGROUND-COLOR: navy;")
$txtstream.WriteLine("   FONT-FAMILY: font-family: Cambria, serif;")
$txtstream.WriteLine("   FONT-SIZE: 10px;")
$txtstream.WriteLine("   text-align: left;")
$txtstream.WriteLine("   white-Space: nowrap;")
$txtstream.WriteLine("   width: 100%;")
$txtstream.WriteLine("}")
$txtstream.WriteLine("select")
$txtstream.WriteLine("{")
$txtstream.WriteLine("   BORDER-RIGHT: #999999 3px solid;")
$txtstream.WriteLine("   PADDING-RIGHT: 6px;")
$txtstream.WriteLine("   PADDING-LEFT: 6px;")
$txtstream.WriteLine("   FONT-WEIGHT: Normal;")
$txtstream.WriteLine("   PADDING-BOTTOM: 6px;")
$txtstream.WriteLine("   COLOR: white;")
$txtstream.WriteLine("   PADDING-TOP: 6px;")
$txtstream.WriteLine("   BORDER-BOTTOM: #999 1px solid;")
$txtstream.WriteLine("   BACKGROUND-COLOR: navy;")
$txtstream.WriteLine("   FONT-FAMILY: font-family: Cambria, serif;")
$txtstream.WriteLine("   FONT-SIZE: 10px;")
$txtstream.WriteLine("   text-align: left;")
$txtstream.WriteLine("   white-Space: nowrap;")
$txtstream.WriteLine("   width: 100%;")
$txtstream.WriteLine("}")
```

```
$txtstream.WriteLine("input")
$txtstream.WriteLine("{")
$txtstream.WriteLine("    BORDER-RIGHT: #999999 3px solid;")
$txtstream.WriteLine("    PADDING-RIGHT: 3px;")
$txtstream.WriteLine("    PADDING-LEFT: 3px;")
$txtstream.WriteLine("    FONT-WEIGHT: Bold;")
$txtstream.WriteLine("    PADDING-BOTTOM: 3px;")
$txtstream.WriteLine("    COLOR: white;")
$txtstream.WriteLine("    PADDING-TOP: 3px;")
$txtstream.WriteLine("    BORDER-BOTTOM: #999 1px solid;")
$txtstream.WriteLine("    BACKGROUND-COLOR: navy;")
$txtstream.WriteLine("    FONT-FAMILY: font-family: Cambria, serif;")
$txtstream.WriteLine("    FONT-SIZE: 12px;")
$txtstream.WriteLine("    text-align: left;")
$txtstream.WriteLine("    display: table-cell;")
$txtstream.WriteLine("    white-Space: nowrap;")
$txtstream.WriteLine("    width: 100%;")
$txtstream.WriteLine("}")
$txtstream.WriteLine("h1 {")
$txtstream.WriteLine("color: antiquewhite;")
$txtstream.WriteLine("text-shadow: 1px 1px 1px black;")
$txtstream.WriteLine("padding: 3px;")
$txtstream.WriteLine("text-align: center;")
$txtstream.WriteLine("box-shadow: invar 2px 2px 5px rgba(0,0,0,0.5), invar -2px -2px 5px rgba(255,255,255,0.5);")
$txtstream.WriteLine("}")
$txtstream.WriteLine("</style>")
```

Appendix B
List of Locales

Below, is A list of locales you can use with your PowerShell Connections. You only need one, obviously, and that will the one for your country.

Name	Locale Code
Afrikaans - South Africa	MS_0436
Albanian - Albania	MS_041c
Alsatian	MS_0484
Amharic - Ethiopia	MS_045e
Arabic - Saudi Arabia	MS_0401
Arabic - Algeria	MS_1401
Arabic - Bahrain	MS_3c01
Arabic - Egypt	MS_0c01
Arabic - Iraq	MS_0801
Arabic - Jordan	MS_2c01
Arabic - Kuwait	MS_3401
Arabic - Lebanon	MS_3001
Arabic - Libya	MS_1001
Arabic - Morocco	MS_1801
Arabic - Oman	MS_2001
Arabic - Qatar	MS_4001
Arabic - Syria	MS_2801
Arabic - Tunisia	MS_1c01
Arabic - U.A.E.	MS_3801
Arabic - Yemen	MS_2401

```
Armenian - Armenia                              MS_042b
Assamese                                        MS_044d
Azeri (Cyrillic)                                MS_082c
Azeri (Latin)                                   MS_042c
Bashkir                                         MS_046d
Basque                                          MS_042d
Belarusian                                      MS_0423
Bengali (India)                                 MS_0445
Bengali (Bangladesh)                            MS_0845
Bosnian (Bosnia/Herzegovina)                    MS_141A
Breton                                          MS_047e
Bulgarian                                       MS_0402
Burmese                                         MS_0455
Catalan                                         MS_0403
Cherokee - United States                        MS_045c
Chinese - People's Republic of China            MS_0804
Chinese - Singapore                             MS_1004
Chinese - Taiwan                                MS_0404
Chinese - Hong Kong SAR                          MS_0c04
Chinese - Macao SAR                             MS_1404
Corsican                                        MS_0483
Croatian                                        MS_041a
Croatian (Bosnia/Herzegovina)                   MS_101a
Czech                                           MS_0405
Danish                                          MS_0406
Dari                                            MS_048c
Divehi                                          MS_0465
Dutch - Netherlands                             MS_0413
Dutch - Belgium                                 MS_0813
Edo                                             MS_0466
English - United States                         MS_0409
English - United Kingdom                        MS_0809
English - Australia                             MS_0c09
English - Belize                                MS_2809
English - Canada                                MS_1009
English - Caribbean                             MS_2409
English - Hong Kong SAR                          MS_3c09
English - India                                 MS_4009
English - Indonesia                             MS_3809
English - Ireland                               MS_1809
English - Jamaica                               MS_2009
English - Malaysia                              MS_4409
English - New Zealand                           MS_1409
English - Philippines                           MS_3409
```

English - Singapore	MS_4809
English - South Africa	MS_1c09
English - Trinidad	MS_2c09
English - Zimbabwe	MS_3009
Estonian	MS_0425
Faroese	MS_0438
Farsi	MS_0429
Filipino	MS_0464
Finnish	MS_040b
French - France	MS_040c
French - Belgium	MS_080c
French - Cameroon	MS_2c0c
French - Canada	MS_0c0c
French - Democratic Rep. of Congo	MS_240c
French - Cote d'Ivoire	MS_300c
French - Haiti	MS_3c0c
French - Luxembourg	MS_140c
French - Mali	MS_340c
French - Monaco	MS_180c
French - Morocco	MS_380c
French - North Africa	MS_e40c
French - Reunion	MS_200c
French - Senegal	MS_280c
French - Switzerland	MS_100c
French - West Indies	MS_1c0c
Frisian - Netherlands	MS_0462
Fulfulde - Nigeria	MS_0467
FYRO Macedonian	MS_042f
Galician	MS_0456
Georgian	MS_0437
German - Germany	MS_0407
German - Austria	MS_0c07
German - Liechtenstein	MS_1407
German - Luxembourg	MS_1007
German - Switzerland	MS_0807
Greek	MS_0408
Greenlandic	MS_046f
Guarani - Paraguay	MS_0474
Gujarati	MS_0447
Hausa - Nigeria	MS_0468
Hawaiian - United States	MS_0475
Hebrew	MS_040d
Hindi	MS_0439
Hungarian	MS_040e

```
Ibibio - Nigeria                    MS_0469
Icelandic                           MS_040f
Igbo - Nigeria                      MS_0470
Indonesian                          MS_0421
Inuktitut                           MS_045d
Irish                               MS_083c
Italian - Italy                     MS_0410
Italian - Switzerland               MS_0810
Japanese                            MS_0411
K'iche                              MS_0486
Kannada                             MS_044b
Kanuri - Nigeria                    MS_0471
Kashmiri                            MS_0860
Kashmiri (Arabic)                   MS_0460
Kazakh                              MS_043f
Khmer                               MS_0453
Kinyarwanda                         MS_0487
Konkani                             MS_0457
Korean                              MS_0412
Kyrgyz (Cyrillic)                   MS_0440
Lao                                 MS_0454
Latin                               MS_0476
Latvian                             MS_0426
Lithuanian                          MS_0427
Luxembourgish                       MS_046e
Malay - Malaysia                    MS_043e
Malay - Brunei Darussalam           MS_083e
Malayalam                           MS_044c
Maltese                             MS_043a
Manipuri                            MS_0458
Maori - New Zealand                 MS_0481
Mapudungun                          MS_0471
Marathi                             MS_044e
Mohawk                              MS_047c
Mongolian (Cyrillic)                MS_0450
Mongolian (Mongolian)               MS_0850
Nepali                              MS_0461
Nepali - India                      MS_0861
Norwegian (Bokmål)                  MS_0414
Norwegian (Nynorsk)                 MS_0814
Occitan                             MS_0482
Oriya                               MS_0448
Oromo                               MS_0472
Papiamentu                          MS_0479
```

Pashto	MS_0463
Polish	MS_0415
Portuguese - Brazil	MS_0416
Portuguese - Portugal	MS_0816
Punjabi	MS_0446
Punjabi (Pakistan)	MS_0846
Quecha - Bolivia	MS_046B
Quecha - Ecuador	MS_086B
Quecha - Peru	MS_0C6B
Rhaeto-Romanic	MS_0417
Romanian	MS_0418
Romanian - Moldava	MS_0818
Russian	MS_0419
Russian - Moldava	MS_0819
Sami (Lappish)	MS_043b
Sanskrit	MS_044f
Scottish Gaelic	MS_043c
Sepedi	MS_046c
Serbian (Cyrillic)	MS_0c1a
Serbian (Latin)	MS_081a
Sindhi - India	MS_0459
Sindhi - Pakistan	MS_0859
Sinhalese - Sri Lanka	MS_045b
Slovak	MS_041b
Slovenian	MS_0424
Somali	MS_0477
Sorbian	MS_042e
Spanish - Spain (Modern Sort)	MS_0c0a
Spanish - Spain (Traditional Sort)	MS_040a
Spanish - Argentina	MS_2c0a
Spanish - Bolivia	MS_400a
Spanish - Chile	MS_340a
Spanish - Colombia	MS_240a
Spanish - Costa Rica	MS_140a
Spanish - Dominican Republic	MS_1c0a
Spanish - Ecuador	MS_300a
Spanish - El Salvador	MS_440a
Spanish - Guatemala	MS_100a
Spanish - Honduras	MS_480a
Spanish - Latin America	MS_580a
Spanish - Mexico	MS_080a
Spanish - Nicaragua	MS_4c0a
Spanish - Panama	MS_180a
Spanish - Paraguay	MS_3c0a

Spanish - Peru	MS_280a
Spanish - Puerto Rico	MS_500a
Spanish - United States	MS_540a
Spanish - Uruguay	MS_380a
Spanish - Venezuela	MS_200a
Sutu	MS_0430
Swahili	MS_0441
Swedish	MS_041d
Swedish - Finland	MS_081d
Syriac	MS_045a
Tajik	MS_0428
Tamazight (Arabic)	MS_045f
Tamazight (Latin)	MS_085f
Tamil	MS_0449
Tatar	MS_0444
Telugu	MS_044a
Thai	MS_041e
Tibetan - Bhutan	MS_0851
Tibetan - People's Republic of China	MS_0451
Tigrigna - Eritrea	MS_0873
Tigrigna - Ethiopia	MS_0473
Tsonga	MS_0431
Tswana	MS_0432
Turkish	MS_041f
Turkmen	MS_0442
Uighur - China	MS_0480
Ukrainian	MS_0422
Urdu	MS_0420
Urdu - India	MS_0820
Uzbek (Cyrillic)	MS_0843
Uzbek (Latin)	MS_0443
Venda	MS_0433
Vietnamese	MS_042a
Welsh	MS_0452
Wolof	MS_0488
Xhosa	MS_0434
Yakut	MS_0485
Yi	MS_0478
Yiddish	MS_043d
Yoruba	MS_046a
Zulu	MS_0435
HID (Human Interface Device)	MS_04ff

www.ingramcontent.com/pod-product-compliance
Lightning Source LLC
Chambersburg PA
CBHW070845070326
40690CB00009B/1711